RELIGION and PERSONALITY

PRENTICE-HALL INTERNATIONAL, INC., *London*
PRENTICE-HALL OF AUSTRALIA, PTY., LTD., *Sydney*
PRENTICE-HALL OF CANADA, LTD., *Toronto*
PRENTICE-HALL OF INDIA (PRIVATE) LTD., *New Delhi*
PRENTICE-HALL OF JAPAN, INC., *Tokyo*
PRENTICE-HALL DE MEXICO, S.A., *Mexico City*

RELIGION and PERSONALITY

Adrian van Kaam, C.S.Sp.
Associate Professor of Psychology
Duquesne University

Prentice-Hall, Inc.   Englewood Cliffs, New Jersey

Imprimi potest:
> Vernon F. Gallagher, C.S.Sp., Provincial
> Pittsburgh, Pa.

Nihil obstat:
> William J. Winter, S.T.D.
> Censor Deputatus

Imprimatur:
> ✠ John J. Wright, D.D.
> Bishop of Pittsburgh

> January 8, 1964

Library of Congress Catalog Card No.: 64-15831

PRINTED IN THE UNITED STATES OF AMERICA
[77321-C]

Acknowledgments

No THINKER thinks alone; no writer writes alone. This is especially true of this author, who is unusually fortunate to live with an outstanding group of scholars and scientists at Duquesne University, whose main interest is the study of human existence. Many thoughts in this book come from dialogue with my colleagues: Anthony Barton, Bernard Boelen, Amedeo Giorgi, Edward Hogan, Henry Koren, Al Lingis, Charles Maes, David Smillie, David Smith, Joseph Smith, Engelbertus van Croonenburg, and Alice Wagstaff. I wish to tell them here of my affection and respect for them and thank them for their help.

It has been my privilege to have had discussions with the many visiting professors who continuously renew the spirit of the Duquesne circle mentioned above: Viktor Frankl, Carl Graumann, Joseph Kockelmans, Remigius Kwant, Dorothy Lee, Johan Linschoten, William Luijpen, Paul Ricoeur, Peter Schoonenberg, Stephen Strasser, and Erwin Straus.

I learned much from the Major Religious Superiors of the U.S.A. when our psychology department held a workshop for them in *Religion and Personality* at Mt. St. Joseph College in Cincinnati. Enlightening also were the discussions with the graduate students of our department of psychology.

I am influenced by the interaction with my friends and colleagues outside Duquesne University especially Medard Boss, Henry Elkin, Gene Gendlin, Kurt Goldstein, Gabriel Marcel, Abraham Maslow, Rollo May, and Carl Rogers.

None of those people should be made responsible for my thought in this area. While they stimulated this thinking they may not totally agree with my slant. My friends and colleagues of a different religious persuasion may be especially surprised about the change of ideas in the light of my theological convictions.

The bibliography at the end of this book will mention the books and papers which were in some way helpful to me.

The Reverend Sisters Helene and Claver of the Franciscan Sisters were so kind as to take the dictation of this book whereas Reverend Sister Mary Aquinas, R.S.M., Chairman of the English Department of Mount Mercy College in Pittsburgh, corrected the grammar. I wish to thank them for their helpfulness and patience. I am extremely grateful to Mother Viola, General Superior of the Franciscan Sisters of Millvale, Pittsburgh, at whose Motherhouse the book was dictated and who in numerous ways facilitated and fostered this work.

Adrian van Kaam, C.S.Sp.

Contents

3 DEVELOPMENT OF THE RELIGIOUS PERSONALITY

4 DEVIATIONS OF THE RELIGIOUS PERSONALITY

RELIGION and PERSONALITY

STRUCTURE
of the Religious Personality

1

RELIGIOUS PERSONALITY AS HISTORICAL PRESENCE

IN ORDER to know how the religious personality grows, it is necessary to consider certain fundamental ideas about the development of human existence. *Existence* in the etymological sense is derived from *ex*, meaning *out*, and *sistere*, meaning *to stand*. Thus *existence* in this context means that it is man's nature to stand out into reality, to participate in being, to be present to all that is. With reference to religious personality, it means to stand out more and more toward God, to participate increasingly in His life, to be present to Him in and beyond all things. When we speak of the development of existence, we must emphasize that this standing out, this participation in God's presence, has a history. In other words, there is no moment in man's life in which his presence to God, to people,

1

and to the world is not changing. Man's presence is always, as it were, in a state of flux. It is always moving—either expanding or contracting, increasing or decreasing, more intimate or more superficial. We know this to be true from our experience in everyday life. For example, sometimes I feel very much in touch with people and things around me; at other times I feel more withdrawn, more inclined to withhold myself. These latter moments are the moments in which I am less happy, less involved, less committed, less alive.

When we reflect on the way in which we feel present to God, to people, and to the world, we become aware that this manner of presence is very much dependent on experiences of our past life. If we felt ourselves to be loved and accepted by our parents at home, it is far easier now for us to be present to God and to the people around us in a trusting way. However, if we did not feel accepted for what we were at home, we are always somewhat afraid that God and the people around us may reject us, dislike us, or condemn us. If we experience this fear, it is very difficult for us to be present to God and to people in a relieved and relaxed manner. Our prayers and our conversation become anxious, more or less formal, stiff and rigid. It is as if we are constantly watching our prayer and conversation so that we may not think, feel, or say something imperfect which may bring upon us the rejection and dislike that we anticipate because of our unfortunate experiences as children.

From this example, it may be clearly seen that man's presence to God and to the world has a history. His history as a man, however, refers not only to the past but also to the future; that is, a man's historical development is influenced, not only by the events in his past life, but also by his reaching out toward the future. The way in which a person is present to the here and now is dependent also on what he strives after for tomorrow. Man is not a powerless captive of his former life. Although it is true that this former life shapes his present involvement to a great extent, it is also true that he can transcend this impact of the past to some degree through the ideals which he hopes to realize in the future. Thus, although it may be difficult for a person to relate to others in a relaxed and trustful manner if his trust was often betrayed in childhood, his ideal of growing toward a more trusting relationship with others will undoubtedly have a favorable influence on his immediate relationships. To be sure, it will not enable him to be at once at ease with others. But it will change at least slightly his perception of them. He may now be able to really experience certain aspects of honest kindness in the behavior of others. This discovery, if it is made over and over again during a long period of time, may finally alter the basic distrust that the person has developed.

The opposite is true, also: if a person does not wish to develop a trust in human relationships, then he will remain the anxious prisoner of his gloomy past. He will be unable even to perceive the kindness, good will, and love in the other. All these human manifestations will be distorted by the impact of his unhappy childhood.

In other words, somewhere a decision of the will is necessary. The person must decide to grow toward a more trusting presence to God, to people, and to the world. The realization of this does not come to him automatically. He must stand out with his whole being toward the future. Only such a standing out from the depth of his existence can save him from the prison of bygone days.

I should stress here that such decision does not mean, of course, that a man is able at once to destroy the wall of his inhibitions, the iron chain of his suspicions. Such decision is only a beginning, a start, a first orientation, the tender bud of a new life. It may take many years, even a lifetime, before this decision is completely fruitful. Therefore, life is only livable if man tries to participate in God's infinite patience with him.

DIFFERENTIATION AND INTEGRATION OF MODES OF PRESENCE

When we look more closely into the development of human existence, we are aware of two movements in this history. One movement is that of differentiation, and the other is that of integration. These two movements complement each other; both are simultaneously present in our lives. They form, as it were, the basic polarity of our existence.

The movement of differentiation is one of discovering and incorporating new worlds of meaning. As we have seen, man is basically present, in many different ways, to God, to people, and to the world.

This fundamental presence of man is more and more differentiated in special presences. A man may be present to art or nature in ecstatic admiration; he may be present to people in love; he may be present to the universe in a scientific curiosity. All these are examples of a differentiation of man's presence to all that is.

This movement of differentiation would disorganize man and tear him apart if there were not another movement that leads to the integration of all these numerous ways of presence and their corresponding worlds of meaning.

Integration leads to unity just as differentiation leads to diversity. Integration unifies and makes whole, whereas differentiation initially breaks up this wholeness. For example, a man may discover God in a new way by discovering a new way of prayer. He may be so absorbed in this new presence to His Lord that he temporarily loses the integration, the wholeness, the balance of his existence. He may be tempted to neglect many important worlds of meaning. He may neglect his study, his daily work, his health. Only a wise movement of integration will enable him to incorporate his new mode of being present to God in the well-balanced totality of his existence as a whole.

Of course, the opposite may happen too. A person may become so enthusiastic about his daily work or study that he neglects his prayerful presence to God. Here again, the differentiation of his existence leads to the discovery of a delightful task or the fascination of study. What is necessary now is not a denial of the importance of the task or the study, but their integration within the totality of the person's religious life.

A man should realize that a dynamic life will always reveal both movements. There will always be a differentiation of experience, interest, and commitment. This differentiation will necessarily lead to temporary experiences of loss of balance at moments when he feels overly excited and idealistic, or overly anxious and worried. This does not matter, however, so long as he gives free play and full reign to the movement of integration. Then, with God's grace, he will be able to give the new world of meaning its rightful place in his life.

It is important to realize that both movements are necessary in an existence that is really dynamic. Sometimes a person is inclined

to escape the tensions which result from the polarity of this movement. He would like to say, "I have reached a moment of integration
in my life; please let me stop differentiating. Don't get me involved
in new interests, new ideals, new worlds of meaning. This will lead
to the loss of the peaceful balance which I have reached, and it
will take time to integrate a new interest or new commitment in
my life. Please don't change me, don't expose me to another environment, don't interrupt my daily habits, don't change my work,
because if you do I will lose my peace of mind." This person is
right, of course; he will temporarily lose peace of mind; he will be
out of his routine; it will take him time to integrate his new environment, his new task, his new study with what he has done for so
many years. However, this is the price which he has to pay for
growth. The only other alternative is to become stale or rusty, for
if he doesn't differentiate his existence he will die psychologically
before he dies physically.

Integration should never be considered as a "thinglike" frozen
state. It does not mean to put things forever in order in a deep
freeze. Integration is a movement, not a thing. It is an activity, not
a state. And this activity can go on only as long as there is something to integrate. In other words, integration as a living, dynamic
movement is possible only to the degree of ongoing differentiation
of our existence. Differentiation and integration are thus interde-
pendent.

We may now consider somewhat more deeply the movement of
integration. Integration presupposes that our different modes of
existence are lived according to some design or plan. It is clear that
we cannot live all our modes of existence at the same time and with
the same intensity. We cannot pray, study, enjoy music, and paint
pictures all at the same time. In short, one mode of being present
must be preferred to another according to the demands of our
reality in which God's will is expressed. At one time we should pray
and not worry about study. At another time we should study and
not be concerned about prayer.

Integration, therefore, presupposes a certain order of preference
in our modes of existence. To say this another way; true integration implies a hierarchy of modes of existence. According to this
hierarchy, one mode will be central in our lives and other modes

will be subordinated to this primary mode of being in the world. For example, a religious person will believe that to love God and to keep His commandments is the most central mode of existence, and that any other mode can be fostered only in so far as it does not oppose this primary commitment to God. This religious commitment does not exclude the other modes of existence, such as friendship, study, love of nature, appreciation of attractive surroundings, delicious food, and pleasant entertainment. All these modes of presence are good for the religious person as long as they do not arrest his growth in his first presence, his presence to the Lord.

Friendship, for example, is one mode of presence. The question may arise whether the special way of friendship or its intensity is compatible with the reality of a person's life. In such a situation, his first obligation is to be utterly honest with himself. He may ask himself: "Is my involvement with this special person really fostering my growth as a religious human being? Or is it hampering my religious and human development? Does it draw me away from the central project of my life? Does it close me off from the voice of God and the voices of others? Or does it open me more and more to the call of grace and the silent appeal of others?"

In other words, it is impossible to make a blanket rule in regard to friendship. My only general guide should be the acquisition of a ruthless honesty by which I plumb the depths of my hidden needs and motivations—an honesty which leads me to ask myself what force is really driving me on? If I lay it down as a general rule that friendship is always good, then I am depriving the individual of his own responsibility for his presence to others. I am giving him a ready-made rationalization that will enable him to escape self-scrutiny. He can then indulge in unhealthy and unwholesome needs under the pretext of the general rule that all friendship is good. I need not even mention that undesirable friendships are morally bad. This is not the question. The real question is: "Is this friendship compatible or incompatible with my friend's or my own human and spiritual growth?" If it is incompatible and I still indulge in it, then I willfully hamper his or my own spiritual growth. I stand still or even go backward in my development. A certain uneasiness, a certain guilt feeling invades my life, burdens my heart, weighs down on my vitality and idealism. The little joys of an incompatible friendship are bought at the expense of the great joy of dynamic living.

On the other hand, it may very well be that I discover in all honesty that a certain type of relaxed friendship with a particular person renders both him and me more open for prayer, for others, and for my duties. Such a friendship is a good thing, at least for the time being. It may happen that after a certain time our personalities or our relationship may change so that our friendship is no longer compatible with our primary commitments. In other words, I can live the life of presence in the right way only when I possess a deep generosity which enables me to be ready at all times to say "no" to any friendship which I clearly understand to be no longer in God's plan for my growth or for that of my friend. If our friendship withdraws us from our duty, from our relationships with others, or from our life of prayer, it is obviously not in God's plan for us. There are times when we may need another person to help us to see this truth clearly, for deep involvement in a friendship tends to blind us to reality.

The influence of a central mode of existence not only prevents the development of a mode which would be incompatible with the primary dedication of the person; it also influences his other modes of being in a positive way. A person who lives a religious commitment as his primary mode of existence will live all the other modes in a different way, for the central mode of being radiates its splendor in all the other modes of existence. The person who lives with God studies and reads in a different way, enjoys nature in a different way, paints pictures or plays music in a different way. All these other subordinate modes of existence are permeated by his presence to God because these other things are done by a person who is primarily present to the Lord. The splendor of this primary presence gives a special beauty and radiance to every other presence. It is as if the richness of this first overwhelming presence flows over into all that the person does or says.

It has been said of the saints that they did all the things that other people do but that they did them in a different way. Nobody could tell exactly what was different, but somehow the activity, the behavior, and the manner of the saints affected others in a special way. Probably the Blessed Virgin never did anything unusual in the village of Nazareth. She lived the simple, everyday life of all the people of her village. She did her daily task like all the other women, but she did the usual in an unusual way. There must have been a special spiritual charm to her words and actions because all her actions were pervaded by her deep peaceful presence to God.

It may now be clear that the main problem of a wholesome human life is that of harmonious integration of the different modes of existence. In order to have this wholesome integration, it is necessary that we be somehow aware of all our modes of existence. This does not mean that we always have to think about them, for this would not be helpful but disturbing. The only thing necessary is that we do not actively deny or repress one or the other mode of being; if we force one mode of being out of awareness then it cannot be integrated within the whole of our project of life. Therefore, we should be aware of even the negative modes of which we may be ashamed, such as our envy, sensuousness, jealousy, and laziness. We may have developed these modes of being in childhood and may not will them now; nevertheless, they are really ours and should be recognized as ours. "I" am the one who is jealous, envious, sensuous, lazy.

I "am" not only my positive but also my negative modes of being. It is only by fully admitting that I am these negative modes of existence that I may be able with God's grace to deal with them. Only then can they enter into a dialogue with the positive modes of my existence. When I know how hostile, how egocentric, or how lazy I am, I can see these activities in the light of my religious commitment. Only then can this religious presence illuminate these dark recesses of my existence. If it does not, I may maintain a split in my personality. On the one hand, on the conscious level, I may develop a beautiful imaginary religious presence; on the other hand, my repressed egoism, aggression, jealousy, and hostility may develop on their own without my even knowing it because I have repressed them out of my awareness.

Persons who strive after religious perfection may be inclined especially to repress the awareness of their gross imperfections. This is due to a misunderstanding of religious perfection. Some people believe that they should be perfect at once; that they should be free of their base inclinations within one, two, or three years. They forget that perfection will never be reached completely. "Striving after perfection" is only a way of stating that they should try to grow more and more in the presence of God in all that they do. These people who try willfully to force themselves into perfection at once sometimes achieve a make-believe perfection, a would-be holiness which implies the delusion of the absence of all possible base feelings, needs, and inclinations. Such a self-deception can succeed only on the basis of a repression of the awareness of all incompatible feelings which are necessarily still there. In this case, the life of the religious person becomes more and more a delusional existence. There is an increasing fixation on little devotions, rigid ascetical customs, external decorum, stereotyped pious expressions. At the same time, there is a decreasing awareness of all egocentric motivations. They grow unchecked like a cancer. Instead of religious commitment influencing egocentricity, the opposite will happen; repressed egocentricity will influence religious commitment. Sooner or later the devotional and pious behavior of the person will be poisoned in subtle ways by his ego-centeredness. He unconsciously will use his external holiness in order to obtain the respect of persons of his environment and he will look down on other people who are not able to maintain such a perfect decorum as he.

PROJECT OF RELIGIOUS EXISTENCE AND LIFE SITUATION

A wholesome religious life, then, presupposes the harmonious integration of different modes of existence. I may ask myself, "What is my guide in this integration? Why do I make one mode of being, the religious one, the center of my life? Why do I keep the others in second place? Does this happen of itself or is there some plan behind it?" We know from daily experience that there is a hidden design in the things we do, the words we say, the phantasies we allow, and the memories to which we give full play. We can even predict to some degree the behavior of the people around us. We know beforehand how certain persons in our environment will handle a given situation. In other words, we *implicitly* believe that everyone is guided by some plan or project, by a certain orientation, a certain style of life.

Human existence is not a blind event like a thundershower or a snow storm. Such events are more or less invariable. Every time they happen we do not look for an individual style and character that will distinguish one waterfall or snow storm from another. Human beings, however, all display an individual manner of reacting to situations. The hidden design, the inner orientation which makes us realize our existence in a personal way may be called our project of existence, our conscious or partly conscious plan of living our individual lives.

This existential project develops very early in life. In childhood our project of existence unfolds in its fundamental form. This basic pattern depends on our aptitudes and inclinations and on our interactions with the people around us, especially our fathers and mothers. This early project of life is not static, or at least it should not be. It should be open to change, to growth, to deepening, and to expansion. Our style of life should refine and enrich itself in the current of our existence, for if we are really open to every life situation we shall continually receive new gifts of insight. These gifts of discernment are lights that illuminate our project of being in the world.

A life situation and its light is a gift of God. Each situation is a sacrament in which I meet His revealing presence. He reveals to me what my life should be when I listen in humility and surrender. Consequently, there is never a moment in which I can say, "Now I know exactly what my life will be." A project of existence is not a blueprint, a schedule, or a timetable. On the contrary, it is a continually changing awareness of God's will for me. If I see my plan of life as a blueprint, I am liable to become very rigid, very stiff, very difficult to deal with. I may become upset if I find myself in a place or with a duty that I did not foresee in my timetable of life. As a result, I am irritated, angry, rebellious, and what I really rebel against is life itself. The human situation changes and no man can predict the change.

God's will and God's presence is incarnated in every changing situation. Therefore, religious dedication to the will of God is not an escape from the adventure of being, from the vicissitudes of human life, from the sudden loss of a fascinating task or an exciting enterprise. Life goes on; new demands are made, and I must go on responding to these demands, no matter how painful, how disillusioning, how disturbing they may be. If my religious project demands that I leave home, I should be aware that in forsaking my home I am saved from its limitations. If I respond generously to the appeal of a strange new environment, I shall develop new aspects of my existence. I shall become a deeper, richer, stronger, more versatile person. When the religious mode of existence is the central mode of my life, I shall encounter in my new situation the face and voice of my Lord. I shall hear the whisper of the Divine in the shattering experience which suddenly meets me, for the eyes of faith see behind the veil of daily life the presence of God.

It is clear that my project of life is a steady growth in the light of God's will as revealed in my daily situation. It may be clear also that the prayer of my existence is the prayer of "Yes, Father," no matter what happens. This "Yes, Father" should be spoken from the core of my being. It may very well be that I do not have illuminating thoughts or soothing feelings when I answer "Yes." Many times my prayer will be only a prayer of the will. Nevertheless, it is the basis of a project of existence that is at once religious and open. This holy surrender of the will is a necessary condition for wholesome spirituality. Any spirituality not based on this openness to "the voice of God in every changing situation" is suspect, for if openness is not present our project of life deteriorates easily into a blueprint or a scheme.

Unauthentic spiritual life is therefore marked by stiffness, rigidity, formality, and inability to move or change. It is as if the "blueprint" person tells God what his religious existence should be. He has it all figured out, and he finds God's will rather disturbing if it does not agree with the plans he has laid so carefully in his novitiate, retreat, or day of recollection. It is true that such a person may genuinely believe that he is following the will of God when he adheres to the rigid outline that he has drawn up for himself for the rest of his life. However, when we look closer we see the fallacy of his notion of God's will. His mistake is not that he is unwilling to follow God's will, but rather that he is convinced that its content is revealed to him completely at a certain moment of his life.

To be sure, there are fundamental features of one's life which one knows in advance; for example, a person who marries knows from this moment of decision that to live with his partner in the best way possible should be a basic and lasting feature of his project of existence. A man who becomes a priest or brother, a woman who becomes a nun knows that when definite vows have been made, the consecrated type of life becomes a central mode of existence. However, marriage and religious life can be lived in countless ways. Both fundamental life situations can lead to numerous social and psychological situations which no one can foresee in detail. Each one of these demanding situations is a new appeal of God to a person to realize his fundamental situation in a new and creative way. Therefore, a fundamental life situation does not close the possibility of growth in his life project; on the contrary, it opens up new areas of unexpected self-realization.

Many people today cannot see their plan of existence in this way. Under the impact of our technical and functional culture, they are inclined to apply to the art of living the same rules which they would apply to the construction or the repair of machines. Unconsciously, they consider themselves to be subtle and complicated mechanisms. When something goes wrong in any well-planned machine, a craftsman is called. Any good mechanic will do. The problem is explained to him. He smiles understandingly, opens his tool box, repairs the faulty situation, and explains exactly how to prevent the same breakdown in the future. When he leaves, the mechanism is in running order.

Such a procedure repeats itself in all technical areas of our lives. We have seen its successful operation from childhood on, when our parents taught us how to deal effectively with the great and small problems which might arise in the use of the tools and gadgets that are a part of the modern home. Is it surprising, then, that we attempt to run our lives with the cool efficiency of an air conditioner or an automatic washer? When something goes wrong, we call in a counselor whom we vaguely perceive as a spiritual or psychological mechanic. We tell him our difficulty and we expect him to smile, dive into his tool box, repair our broken existence, and leave with us a list of technical directions which will prevent another breakdown in the machinery of our lives.

This is a mistaken conception, of course. The art of living differs from the craft of running a machine as darkness differs from light, spirit from matter, or poetry from prose. There simply are no fast and easy solutions to the problems of living. Our existential project is precisely *not* a list of clever technical directions. A counselor in the art of living is the diametric opposite of a craftsman in mechanics. The more mechanical his approach is, the less effective he is as a counselor for human existence. Whereas the first thing to know in a technical crisis is exact information about the instrument concerned, the first thing to know in the problems of life is that we do not know. Life is a mystery to be lived, not a problem to be solved. Before this mystery we stand in awe and surrender. We do not impose our petty categories on the mystery of life; we do not force life into our narrow prejudices; we do not complain that life is too vast for us; we know that life escapes our grasp. We bow in reverence to the mystery of Being; we accept in humility the fact that we cannot understand where life is leading us; we learn the virtue of patience in the school of the adventure of living. For we are like sailors on a ship of unknown destination on an unchartered sea. Very gradually we learn the crucial lesson of existence that we do not ask what life has to give to us, but rather respond to what life asks from us. Then the question is no longer what can I get out of life, but rather what can life get out of me.

This truth assumes infinitely deeper dimension in religious existence. For the religious person, the mystery of life is rooted in the mystery of Divine Providence. Faith in God's project makes it less difficult for the religious person to live with the darkness and uncertainty that are inherent in every human project. He knows that behind the clouds of his own ignorance is the radiant sun of God's presence. This certainty gives to authentic religious existence an air of freedom and carefree relaxation. To be carefree is not to be careless. To be carefree is to be careful in a serene and even-minded way. The freedom of the children of God gives a specific style to human existence, characterized by the peace of heart typical of the authentic believer. This peace is not based on a denial of the darkness and uncertainty of his project of life. Religious existence knows this darkness as well as or even better than nonreligious existence. The religious man, however, has learned how to live with this uncertainty in the light of his faith that everything—even darkness—has a divine meaning, a holy purpose, a mysterious design. Therefore, the first premise in the art of living is to be able to live with one's problems, not to see them as problems to be solved, but as mysteries to be lived. As long as we are anxious, agitated, perturbed about our problems, we prove that we have not yet learned the fundamentals of the art of religious living.

Indeed, each time we attempt to force a solution of our difficulties in a quick, easy way we refuse to enter the school of life. This is especially true of the problems of sin and imperfection. Our personal inclinations to certain types of sin and imperfection will be with us as long as we live. They are rooted in our unique nature and in the dark recesses of our past. To be sure, we must try to overcome them in the current of our existence, but we must also humbly accept the fact that possibly we shall never be wholly rid of them in spite of our efforts. It may be that we must live with a certain imperfection to the end of our life; that we must patiently try to cope with it in countless ways while never succeeding in eliminating it. A certain sin may persecute us until our last breath, humiliate us in the eyes of others, escape our understanding, and fill our eyes with tears. This fact we must accept.

The Lord will never ask how successful we were in overcoming a particular vice, sin, or imperfection. He will ask us, "Did you humbly and patiently accept this mystery of iniquity in your life? How did you deal with it? Did you learn from it to be patient and humble? Did it teach you to trust not your own ability but My love? Did it enable you to understand better the mystery of iniquity in the lives of others? Did it give you the most typical characteristic of a truly religious person—that he never judges or condemns the sin and imperfection of others?" The religious man knows from his own life that the demon of evil can be stronger than man even in spite of his best attempts; he knows that it is the patience, humility, and charity learned from this experience that count. Success and failure are accidental. The joy of the Christian is never based on his personal religious success but on the knowledge that his Redeemer lives. The Christian is the man who is constantly aware of his need of salvation. Acceptance of the mystery of iniquity in our project of existence is a school of mildness, mercy, forgiveness, and loving understanding of our neighbor.

Our existential project is called authentic to the degree that it is in harmony with our life situation. Our project is unauthentic when it is not in harmony with reality as it manifests itself in our daily life. The wholesome person steadily grows in insight into his own individuality within his own situation, and he accepts his personal life with all its possible and actual modes of existence. This increasing self-understanding is accompanied by acceptance of his total life situation. For we cannot separate our life from the situation in which it is lived. We cannot split our self-development from the development of our situation. The moment we attempt to do so, we become unrealistic and unauthentic. At such a time, we begin to dream about a fictitious situation, an ideal state in which it would be possible for us to be perfect. In the meantime we neglect our only possible real growth, namely, growth within the concrete situation here and now. In such a case we enter into an "if only" existence. The person who is caught in the throes of this unauthentic project of life escapes the burden of true self-realization by the "if only" attitude. If only my environment were different; if only I had a more cooperative wife, husband, or superior; if only I were given a different assignment; if only the people around me were more understanding and refined; if only my health were better, my face more handsome, my imperfections more malleable, then everything would be different, then I would be a marvelous person, then I would live a rich and useful life.

It is clear that the "if only" attitude lifts the person out of reality, makes it impossible for him to live a real life, to actualize himself in a concrete sense. He is the eternally absent one, the professional dreamer who never wakes up. His project of existence becomes increasingly fantastic, a castle in the air. The more the person lives in his castle, the more useless he becomes in the everyday situation He becomes expert at complaining because he cannot understand that imperfect life differs from his castle. He is sure that he cannot be at fault, for if life were only like his dream, then he would be perfect. It is not he who is mistaken, but all the others who have ruined his castle. The man of the "if only" existence may travel from house to house, from task to task, from assignment to assignment in fruitless search for paradise lost. He will never find it, and as a result he will never find himself, for we can only discover what we are in the real situation in which we arc.

Therefore, an authentic project of existence should be increasingly in tune with the concrete reality of our assignments; our environments, and the people around us. Of course, this does not mean that we must blindly adjust ourselves to our environment like a wheel inserted in a machine. Such an adjustment would do as much injustice to our tasks and to the people around us as would the escape from our environment into the world of our dreams. An authentic presence to our tasks and to people means that we are present to them not as dead elements but as living human beings. We should be wholeheartedly involved in the immediate developing situation, in the common responsibility, in the shared task. We should contribute our personal insights. Only then can we give our best to the common enterprise, and only then can we receive light and growth from the situation. Frequently we may be tempted not to be present wholeheartedly to the task and to the situation because we have experienced that to be present means to be vulnerable. When we love, we expose ourselves to be hurt. When we interact with persons who are imperfect, we are liable to be disappointed. When we try to realize ideals in human situations, we discover how limited our possibilities are. It is true that these discoveries are painful, but pain is the road to reality. If we respond to reality in the right way, it will not destroy but deepen, fortify, and concretize our project of life. We may describe the growth of human existence as a movement from an idealistic to an increasingly realistic project of being. This movement is not without suffering, but the suffering is far less excruciating once we have accepted its necessity. As long as we remain homesick for the country of our youthful ideals, we shall suffer torment when we wound ourselves on the hard stones of reality hidden under the soft grass of our dreams. As soon as we accept the presence of stones, they will no longer shock or hurt us. We shall dig them up and build a solid house of realistic existence.

A fascinating example of this growth from dream to reality can be found in the apostles. Reading their conversations with our Lord, we are amazed at the lack of realism in the daydreams of these fishermen. They expected to be mighty rulers in a powerful, earthly kingdom. They were so fascinated with their imaginary project that they really fought about who would be the most powerful in the government to be. Later on, they came down to earth and were able to suffer reality for the Lord. What a striking difference between the dreaming young men of Galilee and the practical, mature, older apostles. Consider the incident of the glorification of the Lord on Mount Tabor. They immediately proposed to build three tabernacles in which to retire in happiness for the rest of their lives. Yet these same men, matured, later accepted the trouble of traveling, preaching, listening to endless complaints, and mediating numerous quarrels.

AUTHENTIC SELF-INTEGRATION

If a person develops a realistic project, his plan of life will direct not only his interaction with his life situation but also his self-integration. Reality will teach him which modes of existence he should actualize in his own life and which ones he should discard. There may be a time when his situation compels him to develop a specific scientific or artistic interest. It will then be clear to him that both the reality of his talent and his situation demand that he give free reign to his scientific or artistic abilities. Reality, however, is more than being a scientist or an artist. Life is greater than the fulfillment of any talent. The existential situation in which the person lives may change, and a change in the life situation is always accompanied by a change in the demands of reality. Sometimes the reality of a person's existence is shaken so deeply that central concerns which are dominant in his project of life must be discarded and replaced by others. Take, for example, the exceptional case of an artist who has to leave his canvas for the defense of his country; or a girl who must abandon her graduate studies to take care of her family after the sudden death of her mother. In each case the demands of reality change most profoundly the individual's project of existence.

Such cases are exceptional; but it is true that in every life the integration of the self always implies that the person discard certain modes of existence which are not compatible with a well-integrated and consistent project. To give a simple example: a college boy may develop a mode of existence according to which he enthusiastically dates a number of girls. As soon as he decides to marry one of them, he must give up dating the others. In other words, to attach oneself to certain modes of existence always implies detaching oneself from other modes. All authentic attachment implies detachment. Life implies death. To live one kind of life implies dying to another kind. Attachment is permeated by detachment, involvement is pervaded by mortification, and freedom implies discipline. Freedom and discipline, attachment and detachment, life and death, are two sides of the same coin. One cannot exist without the other. The growth in involvement is always commensurate with the growth in detachment. A person may be hesitant about his decision in favor of certain modes of existence with their concomitant exclusion of others. If so, his project of being will be ambiguous, inconsistent, fraught with conflict, weak and whimsical. Such an ambiguous design of life tears the person to pieces psychologically. He becomes restless; he does not know where he is going; he is the proverbial man who wants to have his cake and eat it too. His life becomes a shapeless, amorphous mass. He is a citizen of many countries who never knows where his loyalties lie.

People become the victims of such murky situations because they lack the courage to decide on one or another type of existence. They are always doubting; they are never sure; they always want to wait until they are more certain, and the certainty for which they wait never comes. There are many reasons for this lack of decision. One of them has been already mentioned: the desire to organize their lives like a scientific experiment. But life is not an experiment; it is a mystery. It is probable that a certain project of existence will mean happiness for people, but they can never be as certain about its effects as they can be when they combine hydrogen and oxygen to form water. There is always an element of darkness, of ignorance, of uncertainty in the decision for a project of life. Therefore, an existential decision is a risk, a wager, a bold adventure.

But man has no choice! Without deciding on one or another

project of life, he shall not really be living, or he shall be the "living dead." He shall be a vacillating nobody, moving about like an unreal ghost. He shall be an inhabitant of no man's land. He shall be like the servant who buried the talents he received from his Master so that he would not lose them. The paradox is that when a man is unable to give up something, he loses everything. If he tries to keep open all possibilities of life, he realizes no possibility. If he is committed to everything, he is committed to nothing. If he chooses all possible life, he chooses death. Consequently, at the basis of a true existential project is the firm decision for certain modes of existence and the exclusion of others. This rejection of other modes of existence should not be a denial of their value. They may be extremely valuable to someone who has chosen to live another kind of life. A person who marries one girl should not deny that he may also be attracted to another girl, but he must decide to cultivate his love for his own wife and not for the other person. Similarly, the person who decides on the religious life must give up the married way of being in the world. He should not repress his awareness of the beauty and happiness which are possible in the marital life. He should recognize that it, too, is a way to God, but not his way.

Very slowly those modes which do not fit into one's project of existence lose their appeal. In the beginning they may still have an overwhelming attraction. This experience is normal and should not lead to guilt, shame, or anxiety. When his commitment is strong and dynamic, however, these incompatible modes no longer participate in his daily self-actualization as fully and continuously as the new compatible modes of life. They recede more and more into the background; every day they lose a little more of their appeal. They are not repressed. They are not forcefully ejected from his existence; neither is their presence denied. They are simply taken for what they are; beautiful, valuable, attractive possibilities of existence which are no longer in harmony with his new, freely chosen design of being. Although good in themselves, they are no longer what God wills for him. Indulging in them in his imagination can only detract from the force and growing unity of his personality. He cannot deny their hold on his life, but he can decide not to foster their development. Admitting their presence is not elaborating their presence. Recognizing their appeal is not responding to that appeal. Admiring their splendor is not becoming involved in their full realization in his own existence. He shall develop the art of appreciating the value of things which he cannot have. There are little boys who cannot see the beauty of an apple tree without giving in to the temptation to steal the enticing fruit. The mature man, on the other hand, can quietly pass by the garden of his neighbor. He is delighted by the beauty of the trees. He is happy that his neighbor will enjoy the apples at the time of harvest, but he no longer feels inclined to climb over the fence and fill his pockets with the fruits of another.

It is of great importance to be able to appreciate deeply the existential values in the lives of others which no longer play a role in our own lives, for if we depreciate them we are dangerous counselors for those who do not share our own style of existence. We unconsciously give the impression that only our way of life is worthwhile. Doing so, we may suggest to others by our behavior that they should join our state of life or that they should experience their own way of living as inferior and empty. Moreover, such an attitude may foster in us a secret pride which inclines us to imagine that we ourselves are exceptional because our state of life is admirable. We may forget that it is not the state of life which makes us worthy, but the way in which we live it. The only thing which God asks of us is that we be faithful to the mode of existence which He has destined for us from eternity. The best state of life for us is the state to which we are called, even if this way of life may be less perfect in itself than others. In short, those modes of existence which are no longer in tune with our state of life should not be pushed from awareness but should very gradually drop out of our existence because of their lack of realization and elaboration. This is the sound way to act. A repression of the awareness of their appeal does not destroy attractive modes of existence, especially when they have played a role in our former lives. On the contrary, they live on in the secret corners of our being. They continue to grow though we are unconscious of them. They evolve secretly, and because we have repressed our awareness of them, they grow unchecked. This process can be explained by the nature of our existence.

We are present to reality primordially in a prereflective way. Usually we do not reflect on the manner in which we experience people and things. We feel, for example, sympathy or antipathy toward a person before we even think about it. It is only when we catch ourselves in the spontaneous movement of sympathy or antipathy that we become aware of our feeling. Only then can we deal with such feelings. We cannot do away with them immediately, but at least we can say to ourselves, "Look how antagonistic I feel about this person. Isn't it unreasonable? Should I not try at least not to give in to my feeling and make it worse? Let me try to see what it is that makes me feel so hostile." The only possible way to cope with unreasonable feelings is to be aware of them, to catch ourselves, as it were, in the act. So long as we are not aware of our spontaneous presence to people and things, we cannot do anything about our reactions to them. A prereflective presence, moreover, tends to grow in one direction. Prereflective hostility, for example, can become an overwhelming power in our lives.

The same is true of those modes of existence which, while incompatible with our present projects of existence, are still attractive and fascinating powers in our unconsciousness. They have grown in our past existence to strong and deeply rooted attitudes. We cannot make light of them. When we deny their existence, we merely make it impossible for us to catch our spontaneous modes of presence to people and situations when they appear in our lives. For example, a playful, easily distracted, lazy student becomes fascinated by the ideal of becoming a real scholar, a man totally dedicated to study, distracted by nothing. This is indeed a worthwhile project, but simply having this plan of life does not guarantee that all of a sudden distractions will disappear. If this student tells himself that from now on nothing can distract him from his new ideal he will deceive himself. He will be diverted from his work without realizing it, for the repression of his awareness of his strong inclination toward distraction will make it impossible for him to catch himself in the act. While writing an essay, for example, he may decide to consult an encyclopedia. Before he knows it, he is losing half an hour in the enjoyment of interesting illustrations. He may even seriously tell himself that he is doing this for his general scholarly development. Such a student will lose hours of time in distractions which he does not even recognize as such. Thus repression of awareness leads to the unchecked growth of that which we repress.

Man is a bodily existence. This means that our modes of existence express themselves in our behavior. Every time that we live a mode of existence in our behavior, we make that mode stronger. If we are faithful to our existential project, then that project becomes flesh and blood. A real incarnation takes place. Our behavior becomes a living manifestation of our hidden design of life. It is written in our words, movements, and gestures. By the same token, if we are loyal to our project and yet open to those modes of existence which, while still strong in us, are incompatible with our project, we shall catch ourselves more and more when these modes appear in our behavior. As soon as we realize their manifestation, we shall stop their elaboration. We shall say to ourselves, "This is enough."

Just as it is true that the free expression of modes of existence in behavior makes them stronger and more available, it is also true that the lack of free elaboration of discarded modes of existence weakens them. They are less and less available, and it may well be that after many years they will drop out of existence completely. A coed, for instance, who was an enthusiastic student of physics may gradually lose this interest when her life project of wife and mother in a large family leads her to actualize the various modes of existence of a homemaker and to neglect the mode of life of a student of physics. This rejection could be a spiteful repression. In such a case, the repressed interest becomes a disrupting force in the woman's existence. But the neglect of her former interest may also be the outcome of a freely accepted new project of being which is in tune with the inherent demands of the reality of her new situation.

In the beginning of the process of integration, one or the other mode of existence which is incompatible with one's ideal existence may still be dynamic and influence motivation and behavior. This is especially true when a whole existential world of associated meanings has been developed in the light of a particular mode of existence. Even one of these meanings is then able to arouse all other meanings of this same world. A rehabilitated alcoholic, for instance, who tries to discard his former mode of life may be suddenly overwhelmed by his rejected existential world if he tastes only one drop of liquor which evokes a whole panorama of past experiences. Similarly, a person who enters a postulate or novitiate may be suddenly disturbed when a certain occasion, such as the visit of the family or the announcement of the wedding of a girl friend, evokes instantaneously the whole world of meaning in which she participated for so long. In other words, the existential project is easily disrupted in the beginning by those former modes of life which are no longer compatible.

In a sense, growing into a new life is dying to the old. This painful death should not be denied. When somebody dies who is very dear to us, we must go through a period of mourning. This experience of mourning is necessary. It helps us to detach ourselves gradually from a past mode of being which was deeply interwoven with the presence of the beloved one. When a person dies who meant a great deal to us, then something dies in us too. Everything in us that was related to the beloved one must die because we can no longer be present in the same way to the person we have lost. The period of mourning is the time in which this dying of a part of us has to take place. As long as we deny or refuse to face this death of self, we keep alive artificially something that should die because of the change in our reality. Similarly, if a new project of existence implies the giving up of former modes of presence to people and things, something dies in us and we must go through a period of mourning. This applies to anybody or anything that has meant a great deal to us. It may be a boy friend or girl friend, or simply a dress that we can no longer enjoy, or a car, or the free use of our time, or the jolly gang at home. The work of mourning is an unavoidable task. We should not feel guilty, embarrassed, or ashamed about it. We should permit ourselves this feeling of loss, and every time we feel it we should renew our decision in regard to our new existential project. Then the work of mourning is not only a painful abandonment of what we once possessed, but also a gradual acquisition of new values, a deepening of our roots in new life. Then our decision becomes strong and solid, and we shall not easily lose our balance when we are reminded of the pleasures

and delights of our former mode of existence. The person who neglects the task of mourning will remain vulnerable and weak in his
new life until he has fulfilled this painful obligation, this consciously taking a stand, this courageous commitment in the face of
what he has to give up.

The task of mourning should not be misunderstood. It is not a
willful, sentimental dulling or self pity in regard to what we must
give up. It means that we recognize and accept the pain of sacrifice which is unavoidable—not in order to indulge in it, to wallow
in it, but to go beyond it. We say to ourselves, "Yes, it is painful to
give up those things, but I do it because it is the will of my Lord."
During the period of mourning, this situation may repeat itself
innumerable times; we will recognize it just as many times and
repeat our existential decision.

The work of mourning helps to cope with the modes of existence
which we have to give up but which are still interwoven with the
fabric of our life. When this work has been done generously, the
pain of dying to our former life will lose its intensity. We may still
be vulnerable for a long time to come. The slightest word, event,
or imagination may bring back at once a world of meaning that we
believed to be dead and buried. However, the impact of such a
re-emerging, powerful appeal will be less excruciating once we have
thoroughly performed the task of mourning.

We shall be like a man who leaves his homeland for a new
country with strange customs and people whose outlook and behavior are very different from his own. In the beginning he finds
it difficult to accustom himself to his new way of life. In the lonely
hours of the night his imagination travels back to the land of his
birth. These are hours of homesickness in which he is more present
to the beauty of the past than to the challenge of the present. However, when he fully participates in his adopted culture, when he
finds a task to which he commits himself, then a new life is born,
a new existence emerges, a new integration begins in which the
customs and manners of his homeland recede while the features of
the new culture etch themselves in his personality. When he returns, after many years, to the country of his birth, he is surprised
to find that it no longer holds for him the appeal of the past. If he
were forced to remain there, he would feel homesick for his new

fatherland, which is now interwoven with the commitment of his entire being. If someone had told him in the first years of his lonely suffering that he would ever lose his longing for his homeland, he would have shaken his head in disbelief.

Something similar happens when a new religious project of existence lifts us out of a world with which our whole being has been woven since childhood. We have lost the familiar surroundings of the past, and we are not yet sufficiently rooted in the strange ways of the world of the present to feel at home, alive, involved, and secure. We have lost the country of our youth, and we have not yet sunk our roots in the new religious situation. However, to the degree that we become involved we shall lose our despair; we shall find peace, serenity, and satisfaction; we shall build a new life which is a new "interwovenness" with the people around us, with the task facing us, and with the customs of the community which has received us. The world of meaning formed by past interests will lose its vividness and attraction in the light of new worlds of meaning.

In the beginning, the dynamic quality of the former modes of existence may generate temporary tension and conflict. The sinner, for example, who was involved in shady dealings or illicit relationships may suffer torture for a long time after he attempts to implement a new religious decision. He will not find a solution to his conflict by blindly satisfying the needs of the past which clamor for fullfillment. Such action will only lead to another and deeper conflict. On the one hand, he is growing in the insight that he must live a new life if he desires to be honest with oneself. On the other hand, he is giving in to past behavior which by its very nature denies what he now believes to be the true and realistic fulfillment of his being. In other words, the person is growing in opposite directions. At the same time, he is running away from himself and back to himself, simultaneously. There is nothing more exhausting, humiliating, and disturbing than such a lived contradiction.

To be sure, in the beginning the integration will often fail. The person will often be taken by surprise. He will find himself back in the old rut before he knows it. But being overwhelmed by the power of habit is not the same as willfully satisfying desires which have been given up. The weakness is not condoned; the failure is not commended. Indeed, relapse is regretted; it does not foster the split but rather bridges the gap between the real and the ideal. The person's recognition of failure as failure is an implicit reaffirmation of what his life really should be. Thus, every failure, even sin and lack of generosity, can be evaluated in retrospect in such a way that it contributes to the wholeness of one's life project. This is the psychological meaning of remorse and contrition.

The latter are by no means only negative attitudes. On the contrary, they are positive orientations, real building stones in the edifice of human holiness. Man is by his very nature not only authentic but also unauthentic, not only saintly but also sinful, not only strong but also weak, not only directed toward God and others, but also closed in upon himself. Therefore, a project of existence must integrate the awareness of holiness and sinfulness, authenticity and unauthenticity, openness and self-centeredness. This means, first of all, that man must recognize his weakness and his vulnerability, the demonic in himself. It is the attitude of humility which safeguards this awareness and makes it a continual structure of man's existential project. Moreover, the unavoidable presence of imperfection, the falling back at times into incompatible modes of being, makes it mandatory to maintain remorse and contrition as attitudes which are necessary if he wishes to realize the only holiness and integrity possible in a sinful existence. Humility, remorse, and contrition should not be experienced as depleting, depressing, negative attitudes. They should participate in the dynamic force, the vigorous joy of his striving toward the light. Indeed, they should be the background against which the splendor of emerging life reveals itself.

When we abolish humility, remorse, and repentance from our lives, we deceive ourselves; we live in a fake perfection; we abandon holiness and integration because we leave out the awareness of the demonic, egotistic inclinations which are as much a part of our fallen nature as our more virtuous, godly tendencies. Our shadow is always with us. And our shadow is more clear and sharp-edged when we walk in the fullness of the sun. The person who grows in the light of grace sees more clearly the darkness of sin. The infinity of light makes him more aware of the abyss of darkness. The saint is the man who walks constantly between two abysses.

No one speaks so eloquently as he of the love and grace of God, and no one laments so poignantly the power of the demonic in his life. Humility and repentance prevent the blind repression of our awareness of those modes of existence which are incompatible with our life project. If we unfortunately repress the awareness of the growth of these modes of life, they will burst forth in dreams and neurotic symptoms; they will generate a conflict between themselves and our conscious plan of life.

Humility and repentance will help us to face and accept the fact that the process of integration is slow, that it is always imperfect and never totally finished. For at all times, certain incompatible modes of existence remain dynamically active within us. They may have lost their crudity, but as a result their expression in behavior becomes more subtle. Even religious behavior may manifest remnants of a former gross mode of life which has nearly lost its force but which still slightly permeates our life.

Religious behavior, for example, may be pervaded by a subtle form of pride. This subtle penetration of spiritual behavior by egotism is sometimes shocking to unrealistic people. Because they are inclined to idealize the human condition, when they meet a good person who leads a life of religious principle they tend to make a little God of him. They forget that human holiness is imbued with human frailty. They should not be surprised that even the behavior of the holiest is tinged with imperfection. They should thank God that the balance of Divine grace and human weakness is slanted in favor of grace. They should be happy that the religious person is still a fellow human being with whom they can feel at home because he shares the weakness of men. It is true that the failures of the good person are more striking in him than they would be in a less perfect life. A spot is more readily detected on a white vestment than on a drab dress. A muddy puddle is more visible in full daylight than in the shadows of night. But it would be wrong to conclude that the whole life of the religious person is therefore unreliable, murky, and deceptive. Moreover, we should be aware that our idealization of a person, our unwillingness to let him have his limitations, may drive him to unauthenticity, may force him to make his life a lie. If he lives what he actually is, the people around him may indignantly protest. Men become bitter when you destroy their pipe dreams and make dust of their idols, especially when you yourself are so unfortunate as to be that idol.

HIERARCHY OF MODES OF PRESENCE

Our project of existence is hierarchical: there is an order among the different modes of existence. Those which are compatible with our religious existential project do not all have the same standing. As we have seen before, the religious mode is more central, more primary, more influential, than all others. The other modes, in turn, have a proper rank too. If I have a true religious commitment, my life is lived for God. This desire comes first. His will is the central light that guides me through the dark sea of life. At the same time, I may have incurred another obligation: I am married. My life is thus committed to my wife and children. Furthermore, I make a living as a career officer in the armed forces. This is a third commitment. In my spare time, moreover, I love to paint. Art is for me not just a hobby, but a true fulfillment of my being. In this example, the hierarchy of my project of existence is quite clear. I love my wife and my children. But the way in which I embody, live, and express my love for them will always be in accordance with God's will, which has the highest rank in my existential project. I am truly dedicated to my military career. However, I shall always take into account the demands of my more primary engagement to my family. If I am ever faced with a choice between a total breakdown of my family and the collapse of my career, I shall prefer to serve my family. Painting is vitally important, but if it interferes with my duties as an officer, I shall relinquish or curtail it. Thus some modes of existence are more central to my being; others are more peripheral and subordinated to the central ones.

A more central mode of existence within a well-integrated life project is always in some way present in a more peripheral one. In the example above, my care for my family is permeated by my love and reverence for God. I see the face of my Lord in the faces of my wife and children. I hear the voice of Christ in their demands. I participate in His divine tenderness for each of them. I make myself the humble servant of Divine Providence in my attempt to help my children to find their own destiny. When I perform my military duties, in the background of my being is the silent presence of my family. I work for them. I am honest, decent, and faithful in order to protect their reputation and their future. When I enjoy painting in my leisure, I do so in order to be a better officer in the hours of my career, a better husband and father at home, and finally a more complete follower of the will of God.

To the degree that my life becomes more integrated, my modes of existence will be more fully permeated by one another. In the beginning, the mutual interpenetration of the various levels of my life project may still be weak. Conflict may be inevitable. I may become so involved in my painting that I neglect my professional obligations. I may become so engrossed in my profession that I cannot be fully and humanly present to my family. I may be so much enthralled with human love in the early days of my marriage that I have no time for prayer. When I finally discover that I am too onesidedly engaged in one or the other aspect of my existence, I may attempt to do justice to the other areas of my life. What may happen then, however, is that I may unfortunately live these various commitments in successive and separate stages. For example, I pray fervently in church, but I do not bring my family, my career, my painting and entertainment with me. I do not live these modes of my life before the face of the Lord. I do not consecrate them in his presence. I leave them outside the church. It is as if I come with a pet dog. When I enter the church, I say, "Lie down. Don't move. I will see you after the ceremonies." But my daily interests, my career, my family are not like a pet dog who would disturb my serene presence to the Lord. They are not separate from me. They are me and I am they. If I never present them to the Lord, I myself am never fully present to Him. I myself am existence: I am "interwovenness" with the people whom I love, with the tasks which I fulfill, with the dreams and hopes I cherish. They all are me, and I am all of them.

The same may be said of the other dimensions of my existence as of my prayer. When I enjoy my family during an outdoor barbecue, the religious dimension of my being is not excluded. For the truly religious man even the family picnic is a liturgy. He is grateful that the Lord allows him and his family to enjoy the happy celebration. He also knows that he is fulfilling God's will when he accepts patiently the less felicitous aspects of the event, such as the screams of little Johnny, the tantrums of Mary, the untidiness of Peter. All of these circumstances, desirable and undesirable, are accepted by the religious man in a spirit of faith. The same is true of his daily professional duties and of his leisure-time activities. Everything is consecrated by the truly religious person. Yet it requires a lifetime to grow in this existential unity. The secret of spiritual life is not so much the art of contemplation in and for itself but the art of integration of life and contemplation, of profession and prayer, of human and divine love, of the profane and the holy.

A religious commitment at the center of a project of existence influences all other modes of life, such as the encounter with fellow men, the fulfillment of duty, the choice of entertainment. No matter what the life project, all the modes of existence influence one another in one way: the central ones radiate their influence to the less central ones, and so on to the most peripheral ones. The whole hierarchy of modes of life ends in the unique and central mode which has been reached by an individual at a certain point of his life. Even when he has reached a lasting central mode of existence, this mode is not static, unchangeable, and closed in upon itself. A mode of life is never a thing, a rock-like immovable substance. If it is real it is always open and expanding, deepening and growing. The religious commitment of a young person, for example, may become far richer and deeper as he grows older and more experienced. Therefore, the integration of his religious existence will show at the same time a deepening of religious commitment and an increasing permeation of the other modes of existence by this deepened commitment. The central mode is comparable to an increasingly radiant heat which penetrates deeply into the less central and more peripheral modes. This explains why and how even the least central modes of existence of a saint manifest that specific quality of religious beauty and charm observed and felt by his contemporaries.

As we have seen, it is always possible in the current of existence that a basic, new, more central mode of being may emerge or that the central religious mode may appear in a new way. An example of the latter appears when a person who has lived a very affective life of prayer discovers a deeper, but less emotional, mode of being present to his Lord. Such a new mode may lead to a restructuring of his whole project of life and its hierarchy. Everything may now be seen in a new light. He may give his companions the impression that he has totally changed. In such a case we speak of conversion. Of course, it is not true that all his modes of existence have changed totally. What has happened is that certain modes have become more peripheral and are now colored by a new central attitude. For another example, a man who once lived the scientific mode as central to his life and later developed the religious attitude as primary may still be a scientist, but science does not now absorb his attention, energy, and time to the exclusion of prayer. His application to science itself may now be more patient and dedicated because of his deep religious motivation. A third example is that of the religious person whose presence to the Lord was first dependent on a multiplicity of small devotions, such as novenas, rosaries, and repeated visits to the Blessed Sacrament. These practices were most helpful to the person at a certain stage of his spiritual growth. Now, however, grace gently moves him in the direction of a more quiet presence to the Holy. The Holy Spirit moves him to be less active, less assiduous, less willful in his prayer life. The central religious mode of existence becomes more receptive. His life begins to resemble a wide open field that is waiting for the Divine dew to settle in its furrows. As a result, his whole life may be restructured, his whole project of existence changes. Less time is spent in novenas. Less attention is paid to the reading of numerous pious books. There is less need now to be occupied in devotional activities. At this moment of existence they would disturb rather than foster the spiritual growth of the person.

Such a change in the religious way of presence to God also gradually modifies the style of presence in other ways of life. A new serenity, a quiet peace, a holy relaxation, sets its mark on all activities and all encounters, for a new presence to the Lord renews all our ways of being. Therefore, when we study the lives of the saints we discover that their whole existence was dominated by concern for the Holy, but that this presence to the Divine was different at different periods of their lives. Because there was a real growth in this presence, their entire behavior developed accordingly. Again, it is most important to realize that the saints were holy and wholesome because their project of existence was in tune with reality. They attempted to move neither slower nor faster than their Divine Guide. The danger is that we, reading their lives, may try to imitate a style of religious existence for which we are not yet ready. If we do this, we are deaf to the gentle whispering of the Holy Spirit to us, and we listen instead to the suggestions of the Holy Spirit to a different person in a totally different situation. At such a moment we are out of tune with reality and we are bound to failure. He who desires to move faster than the Holy Spirit directs him will stumble along the road. His spiritual life will become an illusion, a phantasy that is no longer in touch with his real life situation. If our way of striving after perfection leads to nervous tension, to loss of peace, or to disobedience, we are not moving with the Divine Guide.

ACTUAL RELIGIOUS MOTIVATION

We have seen that man's existence differentiates itself in many modes of presence to reality. We have also pointed out that these differentiated modes find some spontaneous type of organization within man's existential project. We have noted, moreover, that man's existential project is a changing one, and that the impact of this project on his actual modes of existence is likewise always changing. We have emphasized, too, that some of these modes of existence are good tendencies whereas others are negative and egotistic. These selfish modes of existence will always be with him. He can never be totally free of them. But we have seen that even they can serve the wholeness of his existential project if he permits them to lead him to humility, remorse, repentance, and contrition.

My actual motivation within a concrete situation is usually constituted by all the modes of being we have just discussed. In other words, all modes of life which are still to some degree active in me may influence in some manner my existential motivation. My concrete behavior may manifest all of these modes, the good ones and the bad ones. My holiness and my egotism are both present in my daily behavior. Therefore, my behavior is never spotless and angelic. Neither is it merely dark and devilish. My behavior is usually grey. It is a mixture, a blend of the perfect and the imperfect, the holy and the unholy, love and selfishness. All that I may hope for is that with God's grace the holy may prevail over the unholy, the light over the darkness, the angelic over the demonic.

If God is very good for me, behavior may grow toward the light, although never becoming immaculately white. If I am less open to divine inspiration, the grey tends to turn to a darker hue although never becoming pitch black. I am lost, however, at the very moment that I deceive myself into believing that any behavior of mine is either pure whiteness or pitch darkness. When I believe that my behavior is perfect purity, I have closed my eyes to the demonic in my being, which is all the more powerful because I no longer recognize it. When I believe, however, that my behavior is only darkness, then I suffer despair. Even in the worst behavior there is still a ray of light, a potential goodness, a hidden presence of the Lord. Only angels are all pure. Only devils are without hope. But man is the pilgrim who travels between day and night, salvation and damnation. Blessed is the man who serenely accepts the greyness of his daily motivations; who does the best he can and does not worry about the outcome; who is neither overly confident nor desperate.

It is important to realize that our actual motivation is always influenced by many components. We may take for an example a person who has decided to give up drinking alcoholic liquors for love of God. A careful analysis of his behavior may show that a true religious mode of life, a genuine love for God, prevails in his motivation. At the same time, however, we may discover certain other constituents of this motivation which point to other modes of existence, such as seeking to excel, to surpass others, or to belong to a group, in this case, to a group who abstain from drink for religious motives. Further analysis may also reveal the presence of a desire to make a favorable impression on other people. Finally, we may discover that the person also suffers from failure in his career and feels the need to be especially good at something. All these modes of existence, then, play a role in his religious motivation and its consequent behavior.

The latter is a clear example of a genuine religious motivation which, however, is not perfectly pure. But is it not better to have an imperfect religious motivation than no religious motivation at all? People who object to religion because religious persons show mixed motives are narrow minded and unrealistic. Religion does not claim that it changes men into angels. The Church is a church of sinners, not of saints. Religion makes man less a sinner and leads him to the purification of his egotistic motivations. A religion which would claim to make man all-perfect, all-pure would no longer be a religion of this earth, of fallen humanity. Such a religion would be a fake religion. It would be spiritual quackery, a source of illusion, an opium of the mind. The truly religious person is not surprised that his motivations are mixed and ambiguous, that he must live with imperfection, that in spite of his attempts his demon never leaves him, that he abuses holy intentions for unholy purposes. He knows that his imperfections make him the butt of mockery for the unbeliever. But he is not disturbed, because his aim in life is not to appear good in the eyes of others but to be a humble novice in the eyes of the Lord. While he awkwardly tries to be less imperfect, he is joyously aware not that he is spotless but that his Redeemer lives.

When man grows in his existential project, his motivation and behavior become more unified and simple. Many people unfortunately reveal infantile modes of existence in their religious life. A person may be present to God, not God as a loving Father but God as a stern Master. Perhaps his own father was overly strict and he has transferred this image to God. As a result, his whole religious life becomes a childish attempt to placate God, to reassure himself that he is safe, that God will not get him. However, this childish behavior may disappear if the underlying infantile modes of religious life are increasingly discarded and lose their appeal and force. On occasion, however, these infantile modes may suddenly come to life. For example, a person who has long maintained a childish anxiety concerning God and who has finally overcome it may fall back into his mistaken religious perception after a lapse into serious sin. This is tragic, for just at this moment he needs more than ever to trust in the mercy of the Lord.

It is possible that infantile modes of existence may not be discarded, that man may become fixated on modes which are no longer in harmony with the reality of his developmental situation. Some adults unconsciously use childish modes of religious life as an escape from their real life task here and now. Like a child who finds himself suddenly involved in his homework when his mother wishes him to do the dishes, so an infantile religious person may at once indulge in endless devotions when his situation actually demands some hard and realistic decisions. His piety may be a childish escape from study, scholarship, social service, community leadership, professional duties, or hours of dedication to suffering humanity. Such a person needs to grow up religiously, to become aware that the avoidance of daily duty is the avoidance of God, that the primary devotion is the devotion of the life task, that God is found where the suffering neighbor is.

We must realize that it is not easy to change behavior which is sedimented, as it were, in our personality. There is in us a dynamic inclination to remain present to reality in a way to which we have been accustomed for a lifetime. Our basic need for presence, for participation, for existence, may be narrowed to this one mode. The special world of meaning which has developed as a result of this mode of life has become a place in which we really feel at home. We know our way around in this world; we feel secure in its system of meaning. We have developed a heightened sensitivity for everything associated with it. Thus, we may explain those childish and primitive forms of religiosity found in people who in other aspects of their lives mature. They have not grown up in the religious dimension of their personality. To be sure, certain customs may foster this immaturity. For example, childlike religious songs are fine for boys and girls who are receiving their first Communion. However, they sound ridiculous on the tongues of full grown men with heavy baritone voices or of adult women who command responsible positions in the business world. In some countries, customs like these have kept men out of the Church. They have experienced the Church as a dreary place where anemic females and little children sing sweet songs in the romantic light of numerous candles.

Many people are not able to create for themselves wholesome expressions of mature spirituality. If religion is presented to them in the language of nursery and elementary school even when they are middle-aged, we should not be surprised that they remain immature in the realm of religion. We do not find saccharine expression in the language of the Lord, in the words of the Psalms and the Prophets, in the sober beauty of the liturgy. The sentimental, dripping expression of religiosity is an artificial product of a few centuries of Christianity and not at all the authentic expression of mature faith.

Another manifestation of childishness in religious people is the wish to escape the pain of religious sacrifice. They sense that religion means obligation. They are willing to accept the mortification demanded by their life situation. At the same time, however, they attempt to diminish the suffering implied in their surrender of valuable possessions. The only way they can accomplish this is to stultify the awareness of the rich worth of that which they have given up. For example, to be a faithful son or daughter of the Church, of a religious community, or of a lay group for Catholic action always implies the readiness to sacrifice one's insight or judgment if legitimate authority demands it. There are perhaps few things that are so precious to them, so personal and intimate, as their own judgment. Giving up their judgment is giving up themselves. It strikes at the core of their existence, at the heart of their being. It is the free denial of the light which they are. By the same token, it is the perfect expression of submission of all that they are to the will of God. Because this is painful, they may find a way out which will make it impossible for them to experience the suffering of this sacrifice. As long as they do not have insight, do not possess personal judgment, or do not develop individual wisdom, they cannot give them up. The most efficient way to vitiate their sacrifice is thus to remain a child, to become a simpleton, to live as a retarded adult. If they do so, they not only rid themselves of the possibility of ever becoming obedient, but they also make it impossible for their superiors ever to burden them with real responsibility. A retarded adult is rather useless as a religious apostle. A pious moron cannot be put in charge of others.

On the other hand, the religious person who has developed mature insight and is then able to develop the virtue of obedience but refuses to do so is also at fault. Whereas the person who does not possess judgment has reached the developmental level of a child, the one who refuses to obey has achieved the development of a rebellious teenager. Both are of doubtful value for the Church. Both tend to be an obstacle to wholesome accomplishment. It is for this reason that the representatives of the Church today should insist more than ever on the recruitment of only those people who are able to live a life of mature obedience. Otherwise, the workers for Christ will be a hindrance rather than an asset to apostolic endeavors. The Church today must be a response to a modern world with multivarious needs and complex demands. This mature response can no longer be given by religious children or by men and women who are still teenagers in youthful revolt. We need mature men and women who are no longer either inept children without judgment or teenagers who must still show the world that they are no longer dependent. We need people who have grown up to a free and mature obedience.

Maturity does not mean the absence of wholesome dependence. It means only that dependence has changed from a blind, unfree submission to a conscious, free obedience. I choose my dependence freely. Mature dependence is dependent not through lack of insight but because of insight. My deepest independence is that I freely and consciously decide to be dependent. Only that dependence which is a free gift of self honors God. The deeper my insight, wisdom, and judgment, the more I am capable of exercising the virtue of obedience. For I can sacrifice more and feel more deeply the pain of sacrifice. Consequently, growth in the virtue of obedience demands a concomitant growth in my personal judgment, wisdom, and insight. To stunt this development in myself is a secret evasion of the painful virtue of obedience.

RELIGIOUS PROJECT AND CULTURE

The existential project is a personal project which grows organically from man's increasing self-understanding within his life situations. It requires time. Man is not able to develop immediately a personal design of life. As a child he follows the modes of existence which prevail in his environment. He does what father and mother and the people around him are doing. The child thus experiences the world naively and spontaneously. He does not worry about it. He does not question the world or the behavior of his parents and other adults. For him the world is not a problem, a task, or an assignment; it is a simple "givenness." In one sense, the child lives his culture impersonally. His project of existence is more cultural than individual. In other words, he has not yet made his own the cultural values of his environment. They are not chosen or affirmed by him but imitated without question.

As the child grows older, he gravitates toward the adult mode of existence which is characterized by a questioning of one's own experiences. The child now begins to look beyond the world that is revealed in his culture. Therefore, becoming an adult means for the adolescent that he initiates a dialogue between his personal experience of the world and the perception of the world embodied in his culture. His cultural project must become a personal project of existence. It must be assimilated in a personal way. The same may be said of the religious aspects of the project of life. Adolescence, therefore, is frequently a period of conflict between the culture and the newly emerging personal design of existence.

We may describe a culture as the organic whole of the modes of existence which the people of a certain period and country have in common. These communal modes are the fruit of man's standing out toward reality together with his fellow man. This common cultural project of existence, like man's personal project, has a hierarchical structure. We have seen that a personal project embodies itself in man's behavior. Likewise, the totality of communal modes of existence is embodied in a cultural world of language, symbols, institutions, folkways, and customs. Nobody can develop a personal design of life in complete isolation; it always exists in a dialogue with a certain cultural world. Every cultural period constitutes a specific view and a particular project of the world. This project necessarily implies the actualization of certain modes of existence and the consequent neglect of other possible modes.

A child is forced by his culture to participate in the particular ways in which the people of that culture stand out together into reality. The adults are the representatives of this culture who project for and with the child a certain world. Usually, the child obediently accepts the cultural world presented to him. His anxiety, his ambition, and his deeply rooted need for acceptance and approval by the adults compel him to conform. It may happen, however, that certain unique possibilities of the existence of the child differ radically from the modes of existence developed in his culture. The child may then develop disturbances in his reading, writing, or speech. Usually, however, even the disturbed child will manifest an apparent acceptance of his cultural world, even when this world is opposed to his deepest personal inclinations and individual possibilities. This surface acceptance conceals an inner resistance which springs from the fact that he is not at home in the culture. Since he does not experience himself as being tuned in to the common way of perceiving and dealing with the world, he cannot own his culture. He feels like a lost little stranger in the project of human existence. He is an alien in a foreign country.

Such a child may sooner or later attempt to realize modes of existence which he experiences as more congenial. However, he does not find around him existing cultural means and expressions which he can use as examples for the harmonious development of these personal potentialities. A hidden conflict then develops in such a child between his emerging personal modes of existence and the cultural modes. This collision may come into the open when the child arrives at the adolescent stage of his development, for adolescence is the stage of reflection on his own existence and on the cultural world which is offered to him. Youth means expansion, conquest, and transcendence. The most intense personal projection of the world takes place during these years of constantly growing self-awareness. Consequently, the conflict between self-projected modes of existence and those projected by society becomes most acute at this time.

Every cultural period and place develops its own particular modes of religious life. This is even true within the frame of reference of different religions. The particular religious modes of existence are expressed, among other ways, in religious symbols. These symbols are created by those gifted members of a culture who are able to express meaningfully the religious experience of their particular milieu. When such a symbolic expression is successful, it is gratefully accepted by the other members of the culture because it is experienced as a true embodiment of the communal way of living religious values. These symbolic expressions may be rites, songs, paintings, devotional exercises, and religious formulae which are capable of reactivating the religious world of meaning which is inherent in the communal attitude of a culture. These modes of religious life and their symbols may become increasingly one-sided when a cultural period is in its decline. A period of romanticism, for example, may create a religious language which is highly emotional and sentimental. The more rationalistic members of such a culture may feel more disgusted than edified by this kind of symbolic expression.

Many people may never grow to an individual religious attitude; they blindly adopt the cultural stereotypes while repressing or neglecting their personal religious life. This blind adoption may create an unconscious conflict in the religious personality. The more one-sided the religious project of the community is, the worse the conflict, especially when the adoption of this project would imply a repression of strong and unique religious potentialities in the person.

PERFECTION
of the Religious Personality

2

PREOCCUPATION WITH PERSONALITY AND MATURITY

WE HAVE seen how human existence gradually differentiates and integrates itself according to a project of existence. We may now attempt to describe the religious personality once it has reached sufficient differentiation and integration. To be sure, the human personality, and a fortiori, the religious personality, remains a mystery that we can never comprehend. Nevertheless, true personality reveals itself to us under innumerable aspects, in manifold situations. Every new perspective reveals personality to us from a different angle of vision. Therefore, we shall approach personality from various points of view in the hope that our diverse considerations, taken together, may provide some insight into what it is really like to be a personality.

We must always be on guard against a particular danger when we center our interest in personality and maturity. The words *personality* and *maturity* stand for desirable and highly estimable characteristics of Man. If we are not careful, we may be inclined to concentrate willfully and one-sidedly on being a personality or on becoming mature. Such a biased concentration on ourselves can easily become unnatural and unwholesome. It can lead to an unsound "preoccupation" with ourselves at the expense of a wholehearted involvement with God, with people, and with the world. As we have seen, we grow by participation in what we are not. We expand our being, not by becoming immersed in ourselves, but by going beyond ourselves. Truly great personalities—saints and heroes, wise men and mighty leaders—never even think about being a personality or becoming mature. They have no time for such musings. They are too busy writing books, composing music, improving social conditions, organizing new institutions, and alleviating the needs of their neighbors. While doing so with loving heart and open mind, they develop rich personalities without even knowing it. They grow to holiness, wisdom, and effectiveness by responding to the call of their concrete life situation. They would be pardonably surprised to hear of our concern about how to be a real personality and how to become truly mature. They might conceivably say "that sounds fascinating, indeed, but why not go to work? Do something practical that makes a difference among men, and you will see that there is no time left for discussion about the development of your personality. You will be a personality without even thinking about it, and the world will be the better for it." Concentration of attention on the development of our personality may paralyze instead of fostering it. Such studious care may lessen our readiness for participation and our availability to others rather than open us to reality and lead us to full presence to others.

Our activity is generally most efficient when we are totally involved with what we are doing. Then we are not so much thinking about ourselves or even about the way in which we are doing things; we are wholly "out there" where the effect of our action is. As long as we feel obliged to pay conscious attention to ourselves and to the manner in which we act, we are awkward, inefficient, and clumsy. For example, an experienced driver in the thick of traffic does not concentrate on himself or on how to use the brakes or the gas pedal. His whole attention is "out there" beyond himself, beyond the windshield of his car. It is on other cars approaching him and passing him by, on pedestrians crossing the road, on stray dogs emerging from nowhere, on traffic cops and safety signs. The more he concentrates on all of these, the safer his driving is. The more he is present to himself, to the gadgets in his car, the more he is a hazard on the road.

Something similar may be said of our concern with being a personality and becoming mature. Attention to personality at certain times is, however, desirable. Even the expert driver has to be occupied at times with the exact location of the instruments in his car. He had to learn how to use them before he took his driver's examination. Later on, he has to pay attention to his brakes when they do not work or to his speedometer when it will not function. In these cases, a temporary preoccupation with the car itself and with his own handling of it may be necessary. It is clear that a bad and shaky driver and a delapidated old car will require more special care than a good driver and a brand new, smoothly running car. Perhaps the contemporary preoccupation in our culture with developing personality and becoming mature is a sign of a breakdown of personality and the absence of maturity. Increasing concentration of interest in these two essential human characteristics may well mean that humanity is in a crisis concerning them. If we are aware of the dangers of an unhealthy preoccupation with our own personality and our own immaturity, we may profitably consider the religious personality from a variety of viewpoints.

THE PERFECT PERSONALITY IN SELF-EXPERIENCE AND IN THE EXPERIENCE OF OTHERS

Religious personality refers to a personality in which the religious mode of existence is the most central mode of being and which integrates and permeates all other ways of being in the world. The religious personality therefore incorporates all the characteristics of what we may call authentic personality. The only difference is that the religious concern is ultimate in the religious personality—

just as some other concern may be central to another type of personality.

The first viewpoint we shall take in our description of a real personality is the perspective of one's subjective self-experience. How does one experience himself when he is a personality? We should say that the personality has first of all a self-awareness which is rich, broad, and well-developed. This does not mean that he is always thinking about himself. Rather, he experiences a spontaneous presence to his own project of existence. It is usually prereflective, and it does not lead to what we call "self-consciousness" in the bad sense of the word. This implicit presence to oneself implies an awareness of one's project of existence as unique and individual. The personality knows in a preconscious way that he is not meant to be a copy of anyone else, a second edition of his parent or teacher, a duplicate of an admired star or leader. He has achieved true personality and he is deeply aware that he is unique and irreplacable.

The religious personality knows himself as a unique creation with an irreplaceable divine vocation. He knows that God has called him from eternity to be an unique expression of divine goodness, truth, and beauty. If he is a Christian, he realizes that Christ desires to live in him in an individual way. Every Christian personality is a new and special manifestation of Christ that did not exist before him and will not repeat itself after him. Therefore, as long as a Christian is not a personality he has not fulfilled the project of God concerning him. He has not yet given to Christ full possibility of incarnating Himself in a new and surprising way among humanity, for the divine incarnation is a mystery in which each Christian personality participates. Paradoxically, he reaches his summit of participation at the moment that he is most himself and most not himself, in the hour that he is most deeply immersed in Christ and at the same time most personally himself. Being a religious personality is being most truly Christ and most truly oneself. It is a losing of oneself in order to find oneself, and it is a finding of oneself in order to lose oneself. Only when I am aware of myself and accept myself wholly can I give my real self to Christ. If I am a drab and lifeless entity without a face of my own, living a routine existence in mere conformity to the crowd, then I cannot offer to Christ a personal humanity in which he can live in a new and original way. The Christian personality is not a vegetative existence; he is a unique and radiant center of personal thought and feeling. He is a person urged on by the awareness of an irreplacable vocation, a personal mission, a unique presence. Of course, this does not necessarily mean that he does things in peculiar or eccentric ways. It means that he does common things in personal ways, with a personal love, a personal feeling of responsibility, a personal commitment, and in a personal style. He is not a dead element in the community of men, but a personal participant in the mission of society.

The awareness of self so characteristic of true personality is not only an awareness of one's uniqueness but also of one's unity. As long as man is still divided within himself, as long as his project of existence is still ambiguous, split, and broken, he is not a personality. Therefore, to be a personality is the outcome of a long process of self-integration. It is for that reason that young people are not yet complete personalities. They are still seeking their way. They do not yet know where they are going. And even if they do know, they must engage in a long struggle before their projects of life become real unities of compatible modes of existence. Similarly, the development of the religious personality requires time before the person is ready to make the religious mode of existence the ultimate concern of his life. And it takes even more time before such a person can live this religious mode in all the actions and concerns of his life. When this is finally accomplished, the personality has the joyful awareness that he has achieved unity. This awareness gives him strength of purpose, courage in action, and serenity of mind.

The first mark of the experience of being a personality is thus self-awareness in its uniqueness and unity; a second characteristic is the consciousness of one's own limitations, which is the necessary counterpart of the awareness of uniqueness and unity. In self-awareness, a man knows what he can do, the assignment of his existence, the task of his life. In knowing his limits he realizes what he is not. He acknowledges God and His grace as the source of his being, the spring of his goodness, the guardian of his existence. He realizes also that he needs the others who went before him, who are with him, and who will be after him. He needs them in order to survive, to grow, and to make his life meaningful. He is always in need of others. Alone, he is nothing. With others, he is everything. In isolation, he is sterile. In unity, he is fruitful. When he is closed in upon himself, he is without resources and without inspiration, but in community with other men he is inspired and resourceful. The real personality is aware of his own limitations and of his constant need for God and for others.

A third aspect of personality experience is self-acceptance. It is not enough to know one's uniqueness and limitations, one's assets and liabilities. A strong but relaxed and serene personality is based on the wholehearted acceptance of one's unique mission and unique limitations. Only when he takes himself as he is can he be at peace with himself. If knowing oneself is accompanied by self-rejection, then self-knowledge can be horrifying and destructive. Self-respect and self-acceptance are experienced by the true personality. This does not mean that he is proud of himself; rather he respects and accepts the unique but limited task given to him by God. He does not look for another mission; he is not envious of the gifts of the other person; he does not strive toward what he cannot be; he does not blindly imitate an alien existence.

Another mark of the experience of the true personality is self-realization. A personality is aware that he realizes his concrete potentialities within the life situation in which he finds himself. This experience of realizing what he is gives him a feeling of joyful becoming, of healthy growth, of increasing strength. He feels more and more real as a person. This awareness of becoming, however, is in the background of his awareness. It is not the focus of his attention, for the focus of presence in the religious personality is always God, the task, the other, the world. Nevertheless, a feeling of growing "selfness" is a background accompaniment to this experience of presence to the world. When "selfhood" becomes a focus something goes wrong and "selfness" becomes selfishness. In other words, the self closes in upon itself. True realization of the self is always realization in a situation. However, when the experience of self-realization becomes an experience of an isolated self, then the self becomes a fiction. It is man's essence to be existence: it is the very essence of the self not to be self-sufficient but to *ex-sist*, to stand out, to participate in God, in the neighbor, and in the world. This participation is not an accidental thing that may or may not be added to the self. It is an essential constituent of the self. Without it, man does not have a real self but a figment of his imagination. When he concentrates his attention and his energy on this make-believe isolated self, then his real self—which is participation and being "out there"—is not developed, does not grow, and will soon be dehydrated and starved because of lack of the nourishment of reality. The mature personality therefore experiences self-realization in somewhat the same way in which one experiences physical health. When a person is working hard and his body is involved in the task at hand, when he enjoys the willingness and strength of his muscles, the feeling of force and resistance in his whole body, then he does not think explicitly, "How healthy I am," "How well my bloodstream flows," "How marvelously my muscles function"; he thinks only of the work at hand. At the same time, however, he experiences an implicit awareness of his good health and strength. It is only when one feels weakened or ill that one realizes at once that this usual good experience of bodily vigor is missing. Indeed it would be somewhat unnatural and neurotic if a healthy man concentrated continuously on his organic disposition—and so it is with the awareness of self-realization experienced by a mature personality.

A fifth mode of self-experience in the true personality is the awareness of self-determination. The real personality feels that he himself determines his life; that he is not the toy of alien powers. His experience is that he himself in the core of his existence decides what his life should be. This experience of self-determination continuously grows in him. Every day it becomes a little stronger. He serenely performs those actions which are called for by his state of life, by his project of existence, by the realistic demands of his environment. He does not refuse to respond, for he is a committed man. But he knows that he *could* refuse, that he is tempted at times not to respond to the claims of reality. In spite of this knowledge, he freely does what life asks of him. He is at the same time the most obedient and the most independent of men, for his is a free obedience. As we have already seen, the essence of life is obedience. Obedience is derived from *ob* meaning *to* and *audire* meaning *to listen,* so that it literally means *to listen to.* In this sense, it is the

most radical definition of the very basis of human existence: To
listen to the demands of being, the claims of reality, the appeal of
life, the requirements of the situation, is the very basis of his realistic standing out into reality, into being. Therefore, the experience
of self-determination in the personality is a relaxed and joyful
awareness that he himself freely decides to be obedient, to listen,
knowing full well that he could decide not to do so. He is not
obedient because he is forced to, because he is anxious, because he
wishes to look well in the eyes of others, because he desires the
esteem, love, and sympathy of those around him, but because he
freely decides to obey when he can freely refuse obedience. The
religious person who is a real personality is therefore free in the
gift of himself to religion as a priest, a brother, a nun, or a layman.
He is not religious mainly because it is the thing to do in his society,
or primarily because he would be slandered if he did not go to
Church. The gift of himself to religion is a free and joyful offering
of love, not totally determined by custom, routine, or human respect.

The highest human gift is the gift of self in freedom. Only the
true personality who has reached full self-perception can really give
himself in this way. Therefore, another facet of self-experience is
the experience of freedom. The real personality binds himself in
freedom and freely maintains this binding. Freedom does not mean
for him that he childishly shakes off obligations. Rather, he accepts
them because he wills them; he chooses them; he decides *for* them.
The man who cannot accept any binding is not free. He is the victim
of his impulses which may play their game with him and leave him
helpless in the storms of his passions. He confuses freedom with
license. The freedom which the true personality experiences is not
freedom *from* but freedom *to*. It is the freedom to commit himself,
to give himself, to make himself available, to put himself deliberately at the service of One greater than he is. Such a consideration
leads us naturally to reflection on the experience of responsibility.
Responsibility can be read as *response* plus *ability;* that is, the
ability to respond personally and freely to the claims of reality, to
the inspiration of God and the whisper of the Holy Spirit. Only
the mature personality fully responds. The immature personality
can often only react, and this reaction may be blind, uninspired,

automatic, and colorless. The true personality, however, responds with his whole heart and soul, with great love and genuine enthusiasm. He does not *have* a response; he *is* that response with his whole being. For him, as a personality, it is no longer difficult to be that response. One of the joys of his life is his constant experience of his ability to respond wholeheartedly, with the grace of God, to each situation that comes to meet him.

We have indicated various aspects of the true personality as related to self-experience. We shall now consider certain facets of the personality which may be seen by the outsider who attempts to describe a real personality. He is perhaps first of all struck by the originality of life, expression, and behavior of the personality. There is something strictly personal that reveals itself in all behavior of the mature individual. The same is true of the ideas held by a real personality. They are strictly his own. This does not mean that his ideas are opposed to those of others, that he does not share his ideas with a large community of men, that they do not belong to the wisdom of tradition. The originality of his personality implies only that he has assimilated and thought through common ideas in an uncommon way. He has personalized the treasure of tradition. He has made his own the knowledge of his community and society. He deepens this knowledge all the time. He increasingly assimilates it. He applies it wisely in his own life, and he makes it bear fruit in his own situation. It is not a dead, undigested knowledge. It is not a meaningless lump of information. His knowledge, no matter how little or great, is lived knowledge, assimilated wisdom which has become flesh and blood in his personal life. Therefore, even the simple, perhaps small, knowledge which he has always bears the stamp of his own individuality. The person who is not yet a personality, on the other hand, is characterized frequently by an "objective-test" type of wisdom, an accumulation of sterile "yes's and no's." The real personality, however, has an "essay-type" of wisdom which is deeply understood and well integrated within the original fabric of the essay of his life. It is for this reason that the true personality always impresses people with his original expression of the common wisdom which he owns in a unique and individual way.

Another observable mark of the true personality is his wholeness.

His entire behavior shows that this constellation of modes of existence forms an impressive totality, a structured whole. Personality is, in fact, a synthesis of modes of existence which may seem contradictory but which nevertheless form a harmonious totality in the mature person. This totality, implying harmony and integration, leads to the impression that one is dealing with a man who is a perfect unity, without split, break, or fissure. In each aspect of his behavior, one finds deep within him the whole person. His words and his activities are like a melody in which the same theme is taken up again and again. His life is a beautiful composition in which the fundamental theme is repeated in endless ways. He develops an inner richness that is perhaps invisible to the outside world, but which is nevertheless steadily communicated. He is a man who has the courage to live temporarily with positions which are difficult to reconcile at first sight, and which may throw him for the time being into disharmony. However, his basic integrity, the underlying thread of integrated unity in all that he does, inevitably leads to the reconciliation of all compatible modes of existence.

Up until now we have considered only those factors in the personality that present a more or less static picture. Absolutely essential in the true personality, however, is the dynamic tendency. Personality should never be considered as a finished product, a neat package of desirable qualities carefully tucked away in a treasure box. True personality is development, growth, and expansion. This truth may be well applied to the religious personality. The latter is not a state which one achieves once and for all so that one can then sit back in complacency. One can never retire from being a personality. One can never say, "Now it is enough. I have integrated my personality. Now I can relax and enjoy myself." At the very moment that one looks at personality in this way, one is no longer a personality, for one loses the dynamic openness which is characteristic of authentic personal existence. The virtue of the religious personality is like a living flower. When one digs it out of the soil, it withers and dies. Fruit that falls from the tree will grow rotten. If a man's personality becomes only an object of self-admiration, it is like an antique in a museum removed from the living surroundings which gave it meaning. The dynamism of real personality implies a history and an orientation toward the future.

By history we mean here the lively presence of his unique past in everything that he is and does. Orientation toward the future implies his looking toward tomorrow, his ideals, and his realistic expectations. If he is a real personality, both his past and his future are present in a lively way in his being at this moment. This presence of past and future in his decisions of today is characteristic of the religious personality in a special way: The religious personality is increasingly aware of the plan of the Holy Spirit which is revealed to him in his past experiences and in the movements of grace toward certain realizations of his life in the future. His life becomes a fascinating discovery of God's mysterious project for him.

WILL, EMOTIONALITY, INTELLIGENCE, BODY, AND STABILITY

We may now give some attention to the factors which determine various elements of the personality, such as the will, emotionality, intelligence, the body, and stability of action. First of all, let us consider the will. Personality is only personality in so far as life is based not on accident but on insight and free decision. Only a project of life that is freely chosen on the basis of insight is a human and personal project. Only that person can become a personality who is able to distance himself from the many possibilities which life offers to him. *Distance* means here that he does not follow blindly his first impulses, that he knows how to wait, how to delay satisfaction, how to postpone the fulfillment of his desires. He puts, as it were, a psychological distance between an impulse and its fulfillment. In the gap which he creates, he is able to stand still, to think, to consider carefully, to weigh the pros and the cons. It is at this moment of experience that the will enters and can make itself felt. Thus, distance creates room for freedom. This distance is the abode of decision, the beginning of personal life, the principle of personality. It gives the person the opportunity to take a stand toward the possibilities which life presents to him. It is in this freedom that the personality decides what to be and how to be. It is clear, then, that a crucial quality of the will, of the personality, is the constant readiness to distance itself from overwhelmingly attractive elements in a given situation and from impulsive reactions to these elements. This is one of the reasons why the authentic personality keeps his ability to distance himself ready and flexible by means of an ascetical life.

Another constituting factor in personality is emotionality. The true personality never cuts off his ability to feel. On the contrary, his sensitivity helps him to understand other people better. He knows how to listen to his own emotionality, how to use it as a precious source of information. The fullness of personal life would indeed be impossible if he were to repress his feelings and emotions. The affective dimension is a most important one in human existence. It gives the personality its warmth and flavor, its liveliness and attractive spontaneity.

When we speak of intelligence of the personality we do not mean that he should be learned, scientific, or scholarly. A person may be a true personality without any of these accomplishments, whereas someone else who has much scholarly training may not be a personality at all. When we say that a true personality should be intelligent, we mean only that he should have a clear view of the situations with which he has to cope. A clear insight is not muddled by prejudice, anxiety, and impulsiveness, but it has little to do with being learned or scholarly. Many learned men are muddled in daily situations. Many unscholarly women care for their confused but scholarly husbands who fail in their appraisal of concrete situations. A clear, intelligent outlook in daily living is a function of inner balance, serenity, and the quiet readiness to respond to the demands of reality rather than to the fantastic visions engendered by imagination and passion. Paradoxically, learned people often live so much on the clouds of abstraction or in ivory towers of splendid ideals that they are more or less helpless in the everyday environment where imperfect people clamor for solutions of concrete problems and complex conflicts. The authentic religious personality manifests a certain kind of intelligence. He has developed a clear, balanced view of what the will of God demands of him and of others in everyday life. He is not blinded by his own fancy, by his petty prejudices, he is able to distance himself from sudden impulsive emotions. Therefore, he is better able to see clearly what is troublesome in a given situation and what should be done. The religious person who has not become a personality, however, may identify his own unreasonable impulses with the inspiration of the Holy Spirit. He may see his own exaggerated plans and imaginations as the will of God. In other words, he gains in objectivity of insight because of a decrease in subjectivism which was a result of his egoism. It is Grace which increasingly liberates him from the kind of self-centeredness that leads to subjective judgements which distort the perception of reality.

Personality is also to some degree distinguished by its incarnation. One's body, taken not in itself but as a manifestation of inner life, is a genuine component of the personality. Face, movement, gesture, and posture radiate what man is. His uniqueness, his inspirations, his attitudes toward life also reveal themselves in his bodily presence. In the true personality, we see increasing harmony between his personal style of existence and his style of behavior. This harmony, however, must be the result of an organic and spontaneous growth. It is impossible to impose upon a person a style of bodily behavior that is not in tune with his unique self. On the contrary, this artificial imposition of an alien style of action may impede the healthy development of the personality. Sometimes religious persons fall into the error of unauthentic imitation. For example, if a religious person in Scotland were to try literally to imitate the exuberant gestures of an Italian saint, such a Scotsman would appear to his countrymen to be merely an explosive "odd ball" imported from some alien land.

Stability of behavior and action is another qualification of the true personality. He is a man who reveals a certain line of action in his life. He is not moved by all winds; rather, he knows where he is going. Therefore, his whole being breathes an atmosphere of stability, certainty, solidity, and peace. For the religious personality this means that he has finally discovered what God's plan is for him. He has found his own way of prayer, of presence to God. He knows the task which Holy Providence gives him to do. He has found his niche in the history of salvation and he understands and accepts joyfully his small role in the great drama of redemption. The authentic religious personality is the faithful servant who daily fulfills the work of the Lord, and who will be found at his task when the Lord knocks at his door at an unexpected hour. Stability should not be confused with fanaticism. A fanatic is not stable, peaceful, and open, but rigid, tense, and closed. He is fixated instead of oriented. Authentic stability implies the constant readiness to adjust one's orientation when charity, legitimate authority, or daily reality demand such adjustment.

When we review the various characteristics of the true personality as we have described them up to now, we can see them as different manifestations of what personality is when taken in itself. The authentic personality taken in itself is an individual and original person who possesses himself in self-awareness and self-acceptance, which also implies the awareness and acceptance of his limitations. Moreover, personality is unifying and integrating; he develops in himself a unity of past, present, and future, an integration of all compatible modes of existence, and stability in behavior and action. This structured whole of the authentic personality is not static but dynamic: It develops itself in the current of existence by increasing self-determination, freedom, and responsibility in a constant dialogue with concrete life situations.

RELATIONSHIP TO LIFE SITUATION

We may consider personality also from the viewpoint of situation. We have seen that man as existence always finds himself in meaningful surroundings. In what way then, does a real personality relate himself to the life situation? One of the dominant characteristics of his relationship to the world is stability and quiet consistency. The mature personality has found his position in relation to both himself and to the world. He has taken a stand, and this decision consistently colors his attitudes toward everything that happens to him. He is not like a weather vane moved by every wind of change. On the contrary, the basic decisions which the personality has made render him sure and calm on all occasions. Life no longer overwhelms or frightens him. He remains himself in spite of turbulence and disturbance. A real personality is like a rock in the waves of events.

To be sure, even the most mature personality may temporarily lose his poise in adversity. The difference, however, between him and those who are not yet personalities is that he soon regains his equanimity.

This stability does not mean that the personality is unmoved, unaffected, untouched by reality. Indeed, he may be deeply moved by events, while at the same time he maintains even-mindedness. This sounds like a paradox, but a real person is a living paradox, a synthesis of traits which seem to exclude one another. In this case, the serenity in the depths of his being does not exclude profound sensitivity and spontaneity on other levels of existence.

This paradox is most striking in the personality of the Lord. How profoundly He was moved by the suffering of men. He wept over Jerusalem and over the death of Lazarus. He could be moved by holy anger, as when He ejected the venders from the Temple. His encounters with His friends and disciples were pervaded by an exquisite tenderness. In the Garden of Olives He was terrified by the thought of the suffering that was awaiting Him. And still this sensitive, deeply emotional Man maintained in the core of His being an infinite poise, an unshakable serenity, an orientation of perception and purpose that never gave way under the torrents of His feelings. The direction of His will kept the same course in spite of the movements of His heart. His feelings did not change His basic orientation, but humanized the way in which He implemented this orientation in daily life. This synthesis of unshakable orientation and sensitivity of heart is one of the impressive mysteries of the mature personality. As long as he is only one or the other, only rock-like, grim determination or only quivering sensitivity he is not yet mature.

Such a one-sided presence to reality is often a phase in growth toward personality. The religious person who strives after perfection may be sometimes rigid not only in his orientation but also in his behavior. At such times he refuses to pay attention to his own feelings and to the feelings of others. He moves through life with blinders. He looks neither to the left not the right. He is the essence of determination, and he makes many people, most of all himself, unhappy because he does not respect the sensitivity of the human heart. He is like a taut wire of will power.

At other times the immature religious personality may fall into the opposite extreme. He realizes that he should be more open, more loving and tender, more merciful and understanding, but he is not yet able to integrate these traits into a stable orientation of existence. As a result, he loses all consistency. When sentiment moves him, he forgets all about his fundamental duties, his primary commitments, his organization of life. All these seem to melt like snow in the sun when he is deeply touched. One never knows what he will do next when pity, anger, indignation, or desolation engulf him. He is undependable, unstable, vacillating, at the mercy of the moment. Man's greatest danger may be his pity. Many religious persons with lofty ideals have been destroyed by inordinate pity. In helping others, they could find no bounds to emotional involvement. Their unchecked emotionality exhausted their energy and clouded their vision. Finally they found themselves weary and empty, without style or orientation of life. They no longer lived but were "lived by" pity, emotional involvement, and endless anguish about unsolvable situations.

Distance, which is such an important factor in self-fulfillment, is also essential to one's relationship to the world. This distance makes it possible for him to take a stand toward and not to be taken in by his surroundings. For this reason, a personality is never determined by the shifting currents of daily events; he himself determines the manner in which he responds to and deals with the occurrences in his life.

The religious person is anchored in God and His revelation and in his openness to the Holy Spirit. However, the Spirit of the Lord can make Himself heard only if the person creates silence in his existence. By continually renewing his distance from his life situation, the personality is able to create this silence. Only repeated movements of recollection help the religious personality to establish in his life the distance and the silence which are the necessary conditions for a truly personal and creative existence.

This distance, however, is not a "being closed" to reality. Rather, it is the maintenance of a standpoint from which the personality is open toward the world and accepts the world. Everything he experiences means something to him, is a message to him, enriches him. He is completely open to all manifestations of reality without surrendering his interiority, his selfhood, his basic commitment and orientation. The more he is a standpoint, the more he is able to be open to what is, for he can see reality only when he looks at it from a certain viewpoint. If he has no standpoint, idea, or principle, he is lost in an amorphous mass of impressions which tumble over one another without reason or order. The clearer, the more certain and relaxed he is about the commitment of his existence, the more he can look at his situation in a meaningful way.

The true personality, deeply rooted in his primary commitments, feels free and daring in each new situation he faces because he can give himself without fear of losing himself. As long as he is not certain about himself, he does not dare to expose himself to all manifestations of being. He fears that they may sweep him off his feet, that they may destroy the little certainty that he does have. But once he has reached, with God's grace, the fullness of personality he will not feel the same concern. He will be able to really live through diverse exciting events without losing his value orientation.

Of course, he must be careful not to overestimate himself, not to decide too soon that he is a real personality who can expose himself with immunity to all impressions. Otherwise, he will be open to unpleasant surprises. Moreover, it should be added that man never reaches the perfect fullness of personality, that even the mature personality remains vulnerable in many situations. Therefore, one should never lose prudence. Caution itself is a characteristic of the mature religious personality. He knows in which situations he can trust himself and in which he must be cautious. Only the make-believe personality will shout from the rooftops that he can trust himself on every occasion, that he is far beyond the infantile state in which prudence should be his guide. People who shout from rooftops are always in danger of tumbling down and breaking their necks.

The personality who is in this world without being of this world knows how to adapt himself wisely to his situation without abandoning the deepest structure of his existence. He also develops initiative in his relation with the world. In other words, he does not follow after events, but he is steadily ahead of them. He foresees how a given situation tends to develop itself if he is actively and personally present as a participant. On the other hand, he quietly recognizes that his creative participation inserts in the situation a new moment that may change its developmental structure. This participation of the mature personality is dialectical. That is, he does not simply decide once and for all a course of action which he then blindly follows. Rather, he is very much aware that every human situation is dynamic, evolving, always changing in lesser or greater degree. Therefore, he listens to the situation and permits changing reality to influence him; and he in turn influences the situation by a wise response that grows from his dialogue with this unique and living manifestation of God's reality.

Thus the personality is in the situation and transcends the situation. He is a mystery of immanence and transcendence. This mystery received its supreme expression in the divine Incarnation. Christ was in an eminent way immanent and transcendent. Every true human personality, whether he knows it or not, is a shadow of the radiant immanence and transcendence of the Lord. The Christian personality, therefore, can more easily grow to his fullness by a prayerful imitation of his Redeemer.

We may conclude that the personality stands in the world in an independent and stable way, not in complete isolation but in openness and acceptance. He permits the world its impact on himself without becoming a victim of its influence. He finds his own creative response to this influence which he structures out of his own richness, basic commitment, and growing interiority. The personality immerses himself continually in changing situations without losing himself, always emerging from them as a new and enriched human being like the phoenix rising from ashes.

RELATIONSHIP TO OTHERS

Personality may also be considered from the perspective of relation to one's neighbor. In the relation of the true personality to others, we may distinguish three fundamental types of characteristics. First of all, we may look for traits which relate to *being oneself* in relation to other persons. Second, we shall consider the fundamental characteristics which are related to *being with the other*, or reciprocity. Finally, we shall treat of those traits which expressly indicate *transcendence of the other*.

In regard to being oneself in relation to the other, the personality becomes increasingly aware of the uniqueness which distinguishes him from all others who have lived before him, are now living with him, or will ever come after him. The religious person is humbly aware that God calls him to be a unique manifestation of divine Presence in this world.

The real personality is, therefore, reasonably independent of other people. He is able to form his own judgments in respect to the areas of his competence and experience. By the same token, he recognizes the limitations of his competence, experience, and judgment. The person who is not yet a personality may exaggerate one-sidedly in either direction. He may give up his own judgment completely in any area of life, or he may refuse to accept the judgment of anyone else in every thought and action. It is only the mature personality who courageously dares to stand up and be counted when he is competent to judge, but who has also the greater courage of the humble of heart to admit to himself and to others that his judgment is never infallible in his area of competence, and is even more fallible in the far wider areas in which he lacks experience.

The authentic personality is always ready to fulfill his obligation in honor, to defend his rights and his style of existence as long as these do not encroach upon the rights of others. The religious personality knows that his existence is a gift of God not to be buried; it is not a light to be hidden under a bushel, but a candle to shine for many. He experiences himself as the servant to whom God has trusted this unique existence. He knows his duty to defend this divine domain. Therefore, whatever the cost, he will stand in dignity for the unique and precious gift which he is.

His persuasion that his personality is fundamentally a gift, and not his own creation, enables him to grow at the same time in dignified self-defense and in profound humility. This humility is steadly deepened by the insight that he himself fails in some degree to live up to this same personal dignity which he must rescue from encroachment by others. The true personality is a surprising unity of dignity and humility. Again, the most beautiful expression of this paradox can be found in the life of our Lord. Can one imagine a more mysterious blend of humility and dignity than is manifest in the personality of Jesus faced with Pontius Pilate, Herod, and the High Priest? In this respect, Christ is the splendid prototype of authentic personality.

A real personality is not without influence on the lives of others.

He radiates strength and light. His very being is an appeal to the other to be himself, to realize what he is. The inner poise, certainty, and security combined with stability and balanced judgment make the personality a center of quiet in a turbulent world. For this reason, people look to him for leadership and direction. It is, however, most characteristic of the authentic personality that he does not use his influence on the other to make the other like himself. On the contrary, he feels the same respect for the uniqueness of each one of his fellow men as he feels toward his own. His attitude toward his neighbor is a letting-be. He allows the other to become what he is. He appeals to the best in the other. His behavior and appearance, his word and action, stir in the other the desire and decision to be himself in the best possible way and to respond to his own task and situation with the full and humble presence of his own unique personality. Every authentic personality seems to cry out to the other by his very being, "Please be yourself. Realize what God has given you. Be wholly and uniquely present to reality." In this sense his direction is nondirection; his word is rooted in silence, the profound silence of listening with his whole sensitivity to the uniqueness of the other person.

This silence and this listening is even more necessary when the other is still far from being a real person, when he is away from himself, not knowing who he is, walking in the fog, imitating the crowd. He who is at a far distance from himself has covered his uniqueness with thick, grey layers of customs which are not lived in a personal, animated way. His life is not yet a forest of fresh, green trees. It is a collection of dead wood. Here and there, among the dead wood, you may be able to find some promising buds. However, you can find them only when you are able to discard the dead wood of inane conformity. It is the authentic personality who arouses in us the ambition to uncover the buds of our own life, to burn the dead branches, to provide nourishing soil for our own new life by a full and personal presence to reality.

The authentic religious personality knows how to listen to the unique voice of the Holy Spirit in the other who comes to him for direction. His listening is a prayerful waiting for the Holy Spirit to reveal Himself in this person. The spiritual director and the person who comes for direction are both present in silence to the

Holy Spirit. They are centered in the Holy Spirit. However, they attempt to read the inner message of the spirit in the outward signs of concrete reality as revealed in daily life situations.

It may be clear from all we have said that the authentic personality forms others by not forming, leads by not leading, advises by not advising, speaks by not speaking, forces by not forcing. The true personality, in his relation to others, is self-revealing. Without aiming at any form of self-revelation, he is a living expression of the values for which he stands and which he realizes in his existence. Others cannot escape the glow of strength and inner beauty which permeates and animates the behavior of a real person. When you meet him you are always somehow affected, but you may not know precisely what struck you. You leave richer than you came. Something of his quiet self-possession, his loyalty to his life task, rubs off on you. You gain a new confidence, a new hope, a new readiness to become what you are not yet.

This effect is true, in an even deeper sense, of encounter with the religious personality. His unique presence to God, the holy pervasion of all his modes of existence by the divine, his adoring perception of God's will in all situations cannot leave you unmoved. In him you feel touched by God Himself whom he allows to be so fully present in the uniqueness of his personal life.

We have discussed those fundamental traits which are related to *being oneself* in relation to the other. Now we may consider the second aspect of fundamental traits, those which are related to *being with the other* and to reciprocity.

First of all, the true personality is open to the other. No matter how independent and unique he is, he is able to listen to the opinions of others. He knows how to distance himself from himself, how to suspend his own judgment, how to remove himself from his own feelings. This detachment from his own judgment and feeling leads to a relaxed flexibility in the person. His openness makes it easy and natural for him to admit when he is mistaken. He is strong but not stubborn; he is wise but not pedantic; he is unique but not peculiar; he is composed but not isolated. This openness for the opinions, feelings, and attitudes of others does not imply that he always agrees with them. He is likely to give up his own judgment if his openness for the ideas of others makes it clear to him either that he was mistaken or that he misunderstood the situation. But even when he thinks that he must maintain his own opinion, his openness enables him at least to really understand the thought of the other, to really feel what the other is feeling. In other words, he is able to enter the existential world of another person even if he cannot identify himself with that world.

In the religious personality, this attitude leads to a truly ecumenical spirit, a spirit which makes it possible for him to respect the good will of the other and to see things from his point of view. This attitude implies that the religious person learns from all points of view, because his openness prevents him from rejecting wholesale the existential world of the other with which he cannot totally identify. His openness makes him sensitive to any part of that world which he can accept and assimilate into his own personal universe of faith and thought. Therefore, the true personality always expands itself in this open meeting with a variety of people, with a diversity of thoughts, feelings, and attitudes. This attitude is of the utmost importance for the religious personality who is engaged in apostolic endeavors, for openness is the bridge to the world of the other. Thus the religious person is experienced by the other not as an insensitive destructive force, a religious bulldozer, or a spiritual tank unit; rather, he appears as a fellow human being who is genuinely interested in the world of the other, and who in honest dialogue witnesses for his own faith without pressure or condemnation of the other. He manifests in his whole behavior a gentle readiness for an even deeper dialogue in which he and the other may respectfully consider how their different worlds of meaning may be integrated. For the Christian personality, this dialogue is one of the highest expressions of the gentle love and delicate sensitivity which Christ desires to live in every Christian. It may be superfluous to add that the same attitude is characteristic of every educator who is a real personality.

Another trait intimately connected with the true personality is the *assimilative* attitude with respect to others. This means that he is able to take over the opinions of others and to work them through in a unique and personal way. He constantly assimilates new ideas without losing his own independence and his particular stand in thought and action. The person who is not yet a personal-

ity, on the other hand, may be so uncertain about his own identity
that he is unable to listen to the opinions of anyone else. He feels
so insecure about his identity that he must assert himself all the
time, and he does so in emotional and intellectual isolation. He is
gripped by the fear that listening to different opinions may rob
him of the very few opinions which he knows to be his own. Giving up his judgment means to him giving up himself, losing a
prejudice means to him losing his shaken identity.

The religious person who is not yet a personality may reveal
this last characteristic in his own way. He may tenaciously cling
to one type of devotion, one kind of spiritual practice, or one
spiritual director whom he has had for years. He is so insecure
about his spiritual life that giving up any one of his religious habits
means to him the loss of spiritual life itself. He will seriously tell
you that he lost his whole spiritual life when he was changed to
another place, when he no longer had time for a special devotion,
or when he was subjected to a new superior. It is clear that a
spiritual life which is so dependent on special attitudes and opinions or on certain persons is of little worth.

Again, the person who is not yet a personality may fall into an
opposite extreme. That is, he does not oppose the judgments of
others, but he follows the opinions of all without making any of
them his own. He does not really assimilate what others offer to
him. Their ideas do not become rooted in his personal existence.
As a result, he never develops his own face, his own voice, his own
life. His existence is a patchwork of a bewildering variety of ideas,
attitudes, and life styles of countless others. The religious personality who is in this predicament changes his spiritual life with
every new devotion, every new book on spirituality, every new
retreat master. He attempts to become a duplicate of every saintly
life that he reads. He suffers from the illness of spiritual syncretism. That is, he does not harmoniously integrate within his own
spiritual life what is offered to him by spiritual reading, by spiritual directors, and by the saints. Instead, he attempts to assimilate
all these ideas and attitudes and styles of life just as they are. You
may compare his condition with an unhealthy process of bodily
nourishment. A healthy organism can eat a wide variety of food
which is duly assimilated to the organism. When the body is not

healthy, however, many types of food are not assimilated. The person becomes sick and nauseated, and the organism expels the foreign matter, which never becomes part of the body as a whole. Something similar happens to the spiritual life when one is unable to assimilate in a personal way the nourishment presented by spiritual authors and directors.

The Venerable Francis Libermann warns in his spiritual writings against a voracious reading of spiritual authors which does not leave time for personal assimilation. He stresses that the soul should listen first of all to the unique message of the Holy Spirit, that this personal encounter with grace should be dominant in one's life, and that spiritual reading should be only a secondary source of religious inspiration.

Another trait of the authentic personality in relation to the other is a communicative attitude. For the mature personality, it is easy to commune with others. He is mindful to give himself to others generously and gently, but he is also ready to receive. Sometimes his greatest gift to the other is his receptivity for what the other can give him. When he is receptive he allows the other to grow in generosity, to be himself in his goodness to him, to become what he is in his communication to him. The true personality is very adept in the gentle play of giving and receiving. This trait alone makes it a rich experience to be with a true personality, for there are so few who are serene masters of the art of giving and receiving. The religious person lives this attitude in his relation to God. He gives to God himself, his thoughts, feelings, and activities, and he receives from God grace, illumination, and inspiration. Therefore, the life of the religious personality is a liturgy. It is a constant consecration in which his gift to God is divinized and becomes a gift of God to him. The same attitude characterizes the relationship between the religious personality and others. He not only gives from his spiritual richness to his fellow men, but he also knows how to receive from their richness. Their very act of receiving becomes a gift to him, for in their receptance they make him aware of his spiritual vocation, of his religious duty, of his divine mission. The faithful who are receptive affirm by their very receptivity the spiritual fervor and sense of commitment in their priests, brothers, nuns, and lay apostles. Without this gift of receptivity it would be far more difficult for spiritual leaders to maintain their religious idealism, as we know from the experience of those who labor in the apostolate.

A final aspect of the relationship of being with others is the evocative attitude. We have already mentioned this trait in another connection. The true personality evokes in the other that which the other really is. In the presence of a true personality a man does not feel obliged to assume a front. He does not have to play the game of hiding oneself. He can perfectly be what he is and that in a relaxed and easy manner. The coat of social hypocrisy drops, as it were, from his shoulders. This openness makes encounter with a true, generous personality an exciting exchange. To stay with him in the light of unadorned truth is a rich and vital experience. We can observe this evocative attitude most strikingly in the encounters of our Lord. His meetings with the Pharisees, with Mary Magdalene, with the woman of Samaria at the well of Jacob are all marked by a forthrightness which evoked in the others what they really were.

The third aspect of basic traits which distinguish the true personality in his relation to his fellow man reveals him in his transcendence of the others. The true personality is never a colorless member of the crowd. He is not a blind conformist to the mass. He is not taken in by the impersonal "one." By the impersonal one we mean the generalized opinion of the crowd expressed in such terms as "one says," "one does," "one feels," or "everyone says," "everyone does," "everyone feels that way." It is the typical statement by means of which some adolescents, for example, attempt to justify the most unusual behavior. They may say, "Everyone drives his car beyond the speed limit," or "Everyone comes home at three o'clock in the morning." Such an attitude seems to imply that an action is right as long as you can say that everyone does it. This attitude is the perfect expression of mass mentality. It can corrupt even the most idealistic communities of men. If we were to analyze carefully how it became possible at a certain historical period that the Roman Curia and a multitude of convents and monasteries sank to corruption, we should find that the majority of religious persons involved quietly declared, "Everyone does it," or "Everyone says that it is all right," or "Everyone feels that you should not take those things so seriously." The saintly personalities of those times, however, did not join the chorus of dreary voices monotonously repeating, "Everyone says it, everyone does it." Because they were religious personalities, they transcended the Christian crowd, without depreciating their fellow Christians. They tried to understand the weakness of their fellow man, while at the same time soaring beyond the universal mediocrity. It is this characteristic of the true personality which makes him a saving grace in times of decline.

Perhaps we may now synthesize the fundamental traits of the authentic personality in relation to his fellow men. The true personality reveals a uniqueness and individuality which distinguishes him from all others. In this sense he is independent of others and ready to defend his independence in order to remain what he basically is and to safeguard his personal mission in the world. On the other hand, he is open to the other; he is able to learn from the other and to enter his existential world. He helps the other to be what he is, and he communes with the core of the other's existence. He himself transcends the crowd, but his very transcendence is an appeal to the other to lift himself beyond the monotony of impersonal behavior.

RELATIONSHIP TO VALUES

Personality achieves a new meaning when approached from the perspective of values. The true personality is one who has become aware of fundamental values and who is able to view the world in the light of his own value orientation. He has developed, as it were, a fine radar for the presence of values. He becomes increasingly sensitive to every manifestation of real value in himself, in others, and in the world. He discovers goodness, truth, and beauty in spite of their concealment under dreary custom. He is not the "debunking" type, nor has he cultivated in himself the "nothing-but" attitude.

The "debunking" type tears every revelation of values to pieces. He denies the presence of any value. He overemphasizes the sad or ugly aspect of a person, a situation, an institution, or a community at the expense of their valuable facets. He finds great pleasure in expounding the glaring imperfections of his fellow men, and he seems positively sad when a person or a community is praised. He seems strangely to avoid the perception of values as one would avoid a plague or pestilence. He glories in the absence of goodness. The "nothing-but" person, on the other hand, reduces all values, all ideals, all beauty, all greatness, to something that is not valuable at all. When he hears about the success of someone, he is likely to declare that ultimately mere egoism and vain ambition led to the person's achievement.

Perhaps the greatest harm done to the effectiveness of Christian communities is through this disparaging attitude which cannot tolerate the achievements of the other. This may be especially true when such communities are made up of people who live in celibacy. The married person, if his marriage is happy, finds a small circle of admirers who love him and who extol his values and accomplishments even if they are very modest and limited in comparison with those of the rest of mankind. This admiration of spouse and children creates a climate of affirmation and acceptance which the immature person badly needs. But, by choosing celibacy, a man gives up this little community of loving admirers who would unmistakably need him. If he is not yet mature, he may sorely miss this warm affirmation of his indispensability for he is not yet able to believe in his own unique value. He cannot perceive the irreplaceable existence which he is. Consequently, he needs others to repeat to him all the time that he really counts, that he really is worthwhile and needed. But the fact that he cannot believe in his own value will make it impossible for the other ever to satisfy his limitless need for affirmation. It is like pouring water into a bottomless bucket. The person who is so insecure becomes easily upset and irritated when the values of others are mentioned. He experiences the affirmation of the other as a personal attack. It makes him desperate, and he may even feel nauseated. Then, before he knows it, he is decrying and disparaging the value of the other.

There are, to be sure, idealistic communities of Christians who dare to live the life of celibacy and who courageously give up the psychological support of an admiring family in which they are most clearly and unmistakably the needed one. There is only one father and husband, one wife and mother in the family; whereas in a community of men there are numerous fathers, and in a community of women many who live a spiritual motherhood in relation to the world. What an unbelievable intensity of unconscious envy and jealousy can be engendered in such communities if the members are not mature! Then the members are like so many frustrated fathers and mothers, husbands and wives. If one of them gains outstanding affirmation from outsiders or from members of the community, then the others suffer unbearable torments.

Therefore, it is imperative that the members of such communities be real personalities so that they can endure the absence of admiration and affirmation which are given to fathers and mothers by their children, and which husbands and wives or lovers grant to each other as a precious gift. If religious communities are made up of immature persons, it is psychologically almost unavoidable that unconscious envy and jealousy become more pervasive and intense among them than among any other group of the population.

The situation is complicated by the fact that the person who leaves his family in order to become a member of a religious community is usually generous, gentle, and exemplary in behavior. He was outstanding in his own family and even in the neighborhood. As a result, he earned the warm affection and appreciation of the people around him. They let him know that he was unique and admirable. Although he humbly disavowed their praise, he did not realize how deeply he appreciated this constant affirmation by others. However, when he enters the religious community he finds a whole group of people who are generous, gentle, and exemplary. There is no family, no group of acquaintances to admire in amazement his piety and generosity. If he were not generous and pious, he would not be in the religious community in the first place. What was amazing to the outside world is commonplace in religious life. When the person left his home for seminary or religious community, he was celebrated as a hero, an astronaut taking off into space, someone beyond the ken of ordinary mankind. But once the door of monastery, seminary, or convent closes behind him, he finds himself a member of the common run of religious men. The distinction between the admiration of family and parishioners at home and the absence of rare esteem in the religious community easily aggravates the pangs of envy and jealousy when praise is bestowed on another member of a community. In such a situation, the absence of adulation which would be a powerful means to the discovery of real inner values may become temporarily a source of suffering.

Although it is true that we must strive to become mature personalities, aware of the unique value which we are, it remains also true that we cannot force ourselves to be personalities at once. This does not matter, however, as long as we are on the road toward personality. Being on the road toward personality means that we become humbly and peacefully aware of the attitudes which deter us from becoming a personality. Foremost among these attitudes is our inability to perceive our own value and our tendency to begrudge the value of others. This position usually manifests itself in the unconscious envy which we have just described. Therefore, our first self-discovery should be a growing awareness of our possible hidden jealousy. We may have to admit to ourselves without shame and anxiety that we are deeply envious, that jealousy pervades our lives and prisons our souls. Only when we have admitted and accepted the strong presence of these feelings will we be able to cope with them. Once we have transcended our basic insecurity and corresponding jealousy, we shall be spontaneous discoverers of values in ourselves, in others, and in the world. Then the beautiful day will dawn when we may spontaneously feel joy instead of torture when values reveal themselves magnificently in successful fellow Christians.

Another aspect of the life of the true personality is that he establishes a hierarchy of values. He recognizes that not every value occupies the same rank, that a balanced life depends on a balanced system of values. His growing insight into his hierarchy of values enables him to structure his existence realistically. As long as a person has not developed sensitivity for the stress which he should give to various values, he is unable to grow to a well-integrated unity of life and action. To be sure, it requires a long time to realize this insight in concrete life situations. Once it is achieved, however, the personality manifests single-mindedness within a rich diversity of presence to the world. A happy result of this realization of a hierarchy of values is that the personality is a living revelation of the values for which he stands. In this sense, the personality is a real appeal to humanity. He is an invitation to others to commit themselves to the actualization of the values in their own lives.

In summary, we may say that the personality, viewed within the framework of values, is someone who is open to values, enjoys and affirms them in himself and others, and realizes them in his existence according to the hierarchy which is inherent in the values themselves. Moreover, he radiates these values to others, by their very fulfillment in his own life.

EMERGENCE OF SPECIAL CAPACITIES

Finally, we may consider personality from the viewpoint of the emergence of special capacities which have not developed in like degree in persons who have not yet become personalities. This specific development of certain capacities is intimately linked with the various fundamental qualities already described. They can be understood only on the basis of these fundamental characteristics.

First of all, we note a more effective perception of reality. As we have seen, the true personality is less victimized than others by self-centeredness, prejudice, and anxiety. Such unwholesome inclinations and fears may strongly influence a person's perception of God, people, and the world. For example, when he feels deeply insecure he is easily inclined to perceive innocent teasing as an outrageous attack on his dignity. It seems to him that people despise him, underestimate him, ridicule him. In other words, his reality perception is distorted. This is only one example out of many of the warped perception of reality found in the person who is not yet an authentic personality. Such self-centered anxiety and fear render a person far less effective in real life, less practical and exact in the conduct of daily affairs. In the hour of crisis, he is prone to panic. The great religious personalities of the past have been known, not only for their life of prayer and their splendid personal incarnation of the divine, but often also for their realistic management of worldly affairs. This surprising practical effectiveness of the mystic is due in large measure to the fact that he was able to overcome, with God's grace, the disturbing influence of unconscious, self-centered fear and prejudice.

This more effective perception of reality by the religious person enables him to detect more easily the spurious, the make-believe, and the untrue in himself and in others. Thus we may say that he judges people more competently than he did before he grew to authenticity. His clear perception and realistic judgment prevents him from either idealizing or demonizing people and situations. Because he does not feel personally threatened by the defects or superiorities, the liabilities or assets of the world in which he lives, he is better able to perceive people and events for what they are. He experiences no paranoid fright, suspicious envy, or neurotic vulnerability which might incline him to isolate one or the other quality of a person or aspect of a situation and to exaggerate it out of all proportion.

Superiority in the perception of reality in the religious personality also has its influence on his ability to reason, to be logical and orderly in thought. The absence of egocentric concern and its concomitant undisturbed perception of reality eventuate in a mode of thought which is more objective and balanced than that of one who has not yet reached personal maturity. In other words, both the perceptual and the intellectual modalities of existence in the religious personality have reached their peak. Moreover, another result of this improved existential modality is the aptitude to see far more easily than others the fresh, concrete appearances of reality. The mature personality is always ready to experience people, things, and events as they really are with their unique individual characteristics. As long as we are insecure, anxious, driven by self-centered desires, we are less apt to experience what really is. We see things rather through the protective screen of our personal needs, our pet theories, and the views which we have blindly borrowed from our family, neighborhood, or cultural group. We lack the innocent eye that looks frankly and freshly at the manifestations of life. Becoming a personality is removing familial and cultural blinders from our eyes. For the true religious personality, all reality is a fresh manifestation of the possibilities planted by God in the world. Therefore, the person feels that his response should be determined by reality itself and not primarily by his own interests, motives, theories, and past experiences. Instead of a legalistic, categorizing perception, he develops a personal, new

presence to every situation that arises. This does not mean that
he completely rejects categories and laws, but rather that he does
not apply them in a stereotyped manner to human situations. He
does not perceive people merely in terms of a category of law or
ethics. He realizes that the human person transcends every category and that no human situation can be caught in an intellectual
system. This does not mean that he will not defend the law or
apply it when necessary. It means only that the way in which he
applies the law is more human, more permeated by respect and
gentle understanding.

The transcendence of self-centered anxiety, conventionality, and
human respect makes the unknown, the problematic, and the in-
definite less intimidating for the mature person. Insecurity leads
to an exclusive interest in what is safe, sure, and generally accepted.
The true person, however, dares to venture out into the unknown,
the unsafe, and the still undefined if his situation calls for this
courage. For this reason, it is important for religious groups, clergy
or laymen, to have among them many true personalities. Without
these, the life of the group may stagnate. Such paralysis is due
chiefly to the absence of fresh perception of reality as it is. When
such a group cannot experience the uniqueness of changing situations, they are unable to respond in a lively and relevant way to
the needs of their times. Instead of responding, they tend to repeat
the categorical answers given by men of past generations to past
situations. These men are dead and buried; so are the unique situations in which they lived. A religious person who spends his life
closing his eyes to the reality of today and repeating the en-
shrined answers of the past is not alive either. He is in no sense
present to reality. Indeed, he is like a mummy in a museum. People
may venerate mummies on their holiday trip to the museum; may
find it interesting to have museums and mummies around; may
even find it fascinating to observe how people looked and lived
in bygone days. However, mummies do not play an active role in
our daily life. Therefore, the price which the immature religious
person pays for his protection against the perception of reality in
a fresh and personal manner may be very high. The price may be
his own personal life, for which he substitutes the life, perception,

and experience of dead and buried people. The price may also be an abdication of any real influence on society today.

If Christians are dominated by this lack of perception of reality, their impact on the culture is almost nil. Thus great thinkers may cry out that God is dead or that Christianity is buried. Of course, God is not dead; neither is Christianity. What are dead are those Christians who refuse to be present individually, personally, and courageously to their fellow men today, to the contemporary situation, to the struggle of the hour. Their timidity, insecurity, and self-centered preoccupation with their own spiritual perfection cause them to hide behind the veils of conventionality and stereotyped perception of the world.

The perfect example of this situation is the conflict between the personality of Christ with His fresh perception of reality and the self-righteous Pharisees who saw all people, Christ Himself included, through the dark glasses of countless religious laws, customs, and conventions. The Pharisees were probably men of unblemished chastity, of strict religious regularity. They were striving with all their might after religious perfection, which was to them the strictest possible conformity to all rules and regulations. They were chaste but stale, regular but uncreative, pious but closed to reality, lawful but without understanding of human psychology, detached from the world but attached to their own religious perfection. The Lord, with His unconventional fresh experience of people as people and nature as nature, was friendly with the unchaste Mary Magdalene, the rough apostles, and the woman caught in adultery. But He was filled with a holy anger when His path crossed that of the chaste, perfect, lawful, and dignified Pharisees who were no longer able to see other people and the world with the innocent eye and the fresh look, uncontaminated by categories, theories, and prejudices. The Gospel contains a most vivid account of this clash between a religious Person who is a true personality and religious persons whose religion consists in the fulfillment of stereotyped patterns of behavior, to the detriment of personal religious thought, perception, and experience of God, people, and the world.

A most dangerous fallacy would be to consider the Gospel as

merely a history of events that happened long ago. The Gospel is to be read as the account of our situation, of your and my situation. The clash between the creative personality of Christ and the religious mummies of His time is an eternal conflict. In each one of us is both the Pharisee and the true Christian personality which attempts to transcend the lifeless conventionality and dead repetition in our religious life. Christ and the Pharisee are at odds with each other in me. Sometimes I am more of a Pharisee; at other times I am more of Christ. Becoming a true personality means becoming a new man with a fresh, spontaneous perception. It means the death of the Pharisee in me, the emergence of Christ. To a degree, every emergence of a true personality everywhere in the world is a shadow of the emergence of Christ. To be sure, the true personality can attain a Christ-like perfection only when it is evoked and sustained by His redeeming grace.

Another effect of the fundamental attitudes which we have described is the spontaneity, simplicity, and naturalness, the complete lack of artificiality in the religious personality. Because he is not preoccupied with the impression that he makes on others, he does not have to strain for effect. This does not mean that his behavior is consistently peculiar or unconventional. It is true that his fresh appreciation of real values leads him to the insight that many conventions are meaningless, trivial, and superfluous. But he recognizes that they may be important to the people with whom he lives. The majority of men have not reached the level of maturity that is characteristic of the true personality. Therefore, they need a well-structured, conventional frame of living in order to protect them against their own anxiety, insecurity, and timidity. The real personality understands and accepts their predicament. He has no wish to hurt them or to make an issue of every triviality which they cherish. Therefore, he adapts himself graciously to rituals and conventions. However, when convention would hamper a right response to reality in important matters or would inhibit charity and justice toward individuals, then he easily rejects conventional behavior. It is as if the true personality must make a conscious effort to be conventional in those moments when his free, natural, and spontaneous inner life reaches far beyond conventional insights and customs.

A man whose existence is grounded in a truly personal life, moreover, is capable of being strongly focused on problems outside himself. Once he has reached the basic security and trust of the true personality, he is no longer much concerned about himself. One does not find in him the ordinary preoccupation with self that is found in insecure people. He is totally devoted to his mission in life, his vocational or professional duty. When faced with some problem in the current of his task, he can without difficulty enlist his intellectual and emotional capacities in the service of its solution.

A man who is not yet a personality, however, cannot easily engage himself in a task which is not somehow related to the solution of his own inner problems or at least felt to be such. He is usually very select in choosing what he wants to do. His first unconscious question is almost never, "What does this task mean for the common good?" It is rather, "What does it mean for me? Does it make me seem more important? Is there not too much danger that I may make mistakes in this kind of work? Does it give free play to my special talents? Does it not mean that someone else will receive a more significant task than mine? Does this appointment secure for me the affection and appreciation of the people for whom I care?" Of course, these anxious questions are usually unconscious. On the conscious level, they are translated by the fearful person into quite different terms. He will formulate the unconscious question in phrases which sound far more reasonable, noble, and pious than the panicky questions on which his immature existence is built. One can understand the desperate situation of a leader of a group of religious people when many of them are obsessed by the same problem. He must serve the mission of his group, its common task, and its objectives in the world. If he is forced to tailor the task to the insecurities and anxieties of the members of his group, the mission as a whole will suffer and it will be far more difficult to attain the objectives demanded by the contemporary situation.

This is true not only of groups of clergy and religious but also of groups of Christian laymen. These groups must be very careful in the roles assigned to those who ask to share in their objectives. Certain Christians who are plagued by neurotic needs for self-affirmation and self-aggrandizement have not been able to find satisfaction for these needs in their professional, social, or familial life. They may, therefore, unconsciously seek to become important, unusual, and striking in the Church as lay apostles advising humanity what to do for salvation, as liturgical reformers admonishing the clergy to live up to the times, as rabble rousers startling adolescent audiences with revolutionary views. To be sure, some of the goals they strive for may be truly desirable, but some of the ways in which they defend them are neurotic, unwholesome, and immature. They are more concerned with the apostle than with the apostolate, with the revolutionary than the revolution, with the orator than the audience, with their self-manifestation than the manifestation of the truth. Laymen should be engaged in the actualization of religious life in the Church and in the world, but the first task of such laymen should be to grow to true and mature personalities who are Church-centered rather than self-centered, and who have transcended the need for affirmation and admiration by the crowd.

Here again the handbook for the true Christian personality, the Gospel, is very outspoken. The apostles before the descent of the Holy Spirit were immature, self-centered people. They were irritated when people would not shower them and their message with respect and admiration. They angrily asked the Lord to shower, in turn, the cities of such people with fire and brimstone. But the Great Teacher of true personality gently chided them with, "You do not know of what spirit you are." Their spirit was still that of childish, self-preoccupied little men. Later they would receive the Spirit of the Lord which would extricate them from their self-centered existence and lift them to a self-forgetting dedication to a mission as wide as the world.

Another natural outgrowth of true personality is the quality of detachment, the root of which is man's ability to distance himself from his situation and to transcend the crowd. While we have discussed earlier this ability of the mature person to distance himself, we want to stress now the concrete impact of this quality on his daily interaction with his surroundings and with others. The real personality desires a certain solitude which he can maintain not only when he is by himself but also in the turmoil and strain of shared activities. He can remain unruffled, calm, and serene in situations which produce disturbance, anxiety, and excitement in others. Consequently, he is more objective than the average person and able to concentrate to an unusual degree even in the most vexing circumstances. For the same reason, he does not need others in the sense that he must cling to them for admiration, reassurance, and exclusiveness. These qualities may easily be misunderstood as coldness and lack of affection. An example is again found in Christ. For the average individual, it may be difficult at first sight to understand the words which the Lord directed to His worried Mother, "Did you not know that I must be about My Father's business?" Later, at the Wedding Feast at Cana he asked His Mother, "What is it to Me and to thee? My hour is not yet come." At another time, after many people left Him because He had told them that they would eat His flesh and drink His blood, He quietly asked His apostles, "Will you also go away?" To Judas at the Last Supper, He calmly stated, "What thou dost, do quickly."

Such detachment seems unusual to average people who claim, because of their need for sentimental support and emotional exclusiveness, that the personality who detaches himself easily from his situation seems unfriendly or even hostile. However, this is not the case. The personality is truly committed to the other as long as this commitment is compatible with the claims of reality in himself and in the other. His love for the other is more genuine and other-centered than the friendship which is more emotional and exclusive, for this emotional manifestation is frequently due not so much to concern for the other as the other but to an immature need to feel appreciated, loved, and generous. If a person feels insecure in himself and in his own worth, then he feels lost when he loses the other. Because this immature need is rather common among the run of mankind, the average person may be somewhat appalled when he faces the serene detachment of the true personality.

Still another capacity of the true personality is to appreciate freshly and naively the manifestations of goodness, truth, and beauty in daily life. A sunset, a flower, a child, a poem may be thrilling and exciting, not once, but time and time again. The openness of the personality for reality leads to this ecstasy springing from the basic experiences of his life. He would not feel the same joy in winning sums of money, participating in a wild party, attending a cheap movie, or being praised for superficial possessions.

This ability to appreciate makes daily life a source of joy for the real personality. Many times a day he is re-created without seeking recreation. This quality is infinitely deepened and enhanced in the religious personality. For him simple manifestations of goodness, truth, and beauty are revelations of God Himself. Many times a day he breaks forth in a spontaneous act of thanksgiving when he is moved to the core of his being by the presence of God in the good things of daily life. He feels steadily transformed and strengthened by such experiences.

The true personality is also ecumenical in his feeling. We use the word *ecumenical* in the widest sense, meaning that the religious person deeply experiences sympathy and affection for all human beings. He easily and spontaneously identifies himself with all men regardless of creed, culture, color, or nationality. While he may be saddened and irritated by the foolish behavior of others, he nevertheless easily feels a kinship with them. This experience of brotherhood is deepened in the religious person by his conscious awareness of the Fatherhood of God and of our common redemption by Christ.

This serious lover of all men is not without a sense of humor. To be sure, he need not be an accomplished jokester or a clever manipulator of words. His is a very subtle kind of humor far removed from the superficially comic. It is more an attitude in depth than a skill in witty remarks. Such existential humor is rooted in the personality's detachment from his life situation. This distance makes him easily aware of the amusing disproportion between the make-believe attitudes of himself and others and sober reality. In this sense, every saint is potentially a humorist even if he appears rather sober and serious to those unable to understand his humor. The late Pope John XXIII provides an apt illustration of the humor of detachment. Most of his legendary remarks reveal his gentle pleasure when people around him made a bustle and stir over trifles.

Creativeness and originality always marks the true personality. He need not be a genius, nor even possess the very special talents with which certain people are born. The creativity of the true personality is linked to the fresh, naive, direct perception of reality which we have mentioned in the description of the fundamental traits of the personality. This freshness of outlook leads to personal insights which are more penetrating and original than those of people who are not yet personalities. The daily concrete expression of this creativeness may even be very simple and humble. The person may be a creative cook or gardener. Everything he does, he does creatively. When he performs his task, not in a stereotyped, stale, and monotonous manner but with the full presence of his personality, he is truly creative. He is surprised by his own inventiveness. Such creativeness gives zest to life, animation to daily work, freshness and joy even to occupations which would otherwise bring only boredom.

SUMMARY OF THE CHARACTERISTICS OF THE PERFECT RELIGIOUS PERSONALITY

We have considered the personality from a variety of viewpoints. To be sure, all these perspectives describe the same identical reality, but each perspective reveals many aspects. The variety of characteristics which we have discovered do not exclude but complement one another. We may now conclude that the true personality in its various qualifications appears to us as totally unique, revealing itself to the other in its own modes, modalities, hierarchy, and style of existence. Not only is this uniqueness present in fact, but the personality himself is increasingly aware of the irreplaceable individuality of his existence. This implies that he also knows the meaning of his life, the orientation of his personal being. To be sure, he is not at once or even ever totally aware of the full meaning of his unique existence because his individuality is always developing; it is never fully present and completed like a material product. What the person actually knows about himself implies his past and points to his future. Both the recollection and the anticipation are part of the self-understanding of the personality.

The personality grows to this self-understanding by his encounter with God, people, and the world. The person as existence knows himself from the way in which the world appears to him, for, as we have seen, the world is not something totally outside himself; it is that to which he is oriented. The life situation is the region in which and toward which he must increasingly become himself. This existential self-realization in and through the world is a task to which the person is committed, and which develops according to a project of existence which is not a stale and finished blueprint but a growing insight into what his life should be.

The encounter between the personality and the world actualizes many modes of existence. As the person develops, some modes of existence may seem incompatible with one another. He accepts this seeming incompatibility temporarily, however, until he is able to reconcile the different modes of existence from a higher viewpoint. The highest mode of existence for the religious person is commitment to the divine.

The real personality is thus a totality which harmoniously integrates a multiplicity of modes of existence, but he is by no means a "closed system." He is always open to further development. Man comes to be himself in and through the world and in and through the other. The other, however, is not merely a means to one's self-actualization. On the contrary, the more someone becomes a personality, the more he is able to evoke in the other the same modes of being. It is only in a meeting between two people who are really themselves that a full human communion becomes possible.

There are two dangers in becoming oneself in and through the other and the world. On the one hand, a person may be tempted in the process to close in upon himself, to isolate himself from the world. This response would sooner or later lead to stagnation in self-development. On the other hand, the person may be inclined to lose himself totally in the world. This reaction also would make real growth of self impossible, for there would be no real self that could develop. There is no complete fusion possible between person and world. The person projects his world, but this project implies his transcendence of the world. This transcendence is possible because of man's intelligence which lifts him from the limitations of time and space. Moreover, his will enables him to distance himself from that which attracts or repels him in his situation.

The personality is never imprisoned totally in his past, for he can anticipate his future and from this future he can impose a new meaning on the past. For example, a boy who once lived in a slum may decide that his past should mean to him that he should destroy that society which tolerated slums. On the other hand, he may just as well grow to the existential decision that he will become a man who by his education, idealism, and practical organization will help to abolish slums in his city. Nor is the personality totally imprisoned by the here and now of the life situation, for he is able to envision the absolute and the infinite behind the veils of the momentary and the incidental. It is for all these reasons that man is independent, free, and responsible while at the same time limited and dependent in respect to eternal values of which he himself becomes the humble manifestation.

As we began our discussions concerning maturity and personality with a warning, we shall conclude by cautioning against possible misunderstandings. When we survey the various characteristics of personality, we easily distinguish two different classes of qualities. We are faced first with a group of fundamental primary traits. They form, as it were, the necessary constituents of the mature personality. Next we find another group of traits which we may call secondary and which are by no means necessary for one to be a personality, traits such as being impressive, appreciated, successful, well-liked, talented, or famous. These traits may or may not be found in a personality. They in themselves do not make the personality. They are only incidental manifestations of one who happens to be in a life situation which is favorable either to his recognition by others or to the development of his specific abilities.

Existentially speaking, however, the most fundamental characteristic of the true personality is constant readiness to respond fully to the demands of reality. Sometimes this response may imply the full development of his specific skills and abilities. If this is the case, he will develop these capacities to the utmost. He will place no limit to the actualization of his talents. On the other hand, such development of talent may sometimes be incompatible with the demands of one's life situation. Certainly we should never say, for example, that the numerous fathers and mothers with low incomes and large families cannot live personal lives simply because they have neither the time nor the resources to develop one or the other specific ability. Rather, we must say that following such an ambition at the expense of the welfare of their families would make it impossible for them to become real personalities in the primary sense. A mother who would neglect her children because she desires time and money to pursue her special interest in painting, or even church activities, would be unfaithful to the demands of her life situation. Instead of becoming a unique personality, she would deteriorate into a disintegrated, egocentric person, constantly repressing the pangs of existential guilt over the betrayal of her vocation.

PRIMARY AND SECONDARY PERSONALITY; CHARACTER AND TEMPERAMENT

The example just cited illustrates how the reversal of primary and secondary personality characteristics can be disastrous. This is also true for the religious person. One who has dedicated his life to religion should develop all his specific talents enthusiastically when they can be used in the service of his life task. He should even inform his responsible superiors that he feels an inclination for a special study, training, or occupation. The superiors in turn have a grave responsibility to foster this development if possible and to put such talents into the service of the Church and humanity.

However, if the mission of the religious group concerned makes it impossible to foster such development, the superior should ask the person to sacrifice his special capacities. Or he should be advised to enter another religious group where there is need for such specific abilities because of the particular objectives of that institute. For nearly all persons in all professions, however, whether in marriage, in clerical and religious life, or in the lay apostolate, it will be necessary to sacrifice the development of certain abilities. It is seldom that a life situation and its demands will form a one-to-one correspondence with all the specific talents which an individual would like to develop to their full height.

Especially in religious communities, the ambition to develop one's own special talent may lead to bitterness in the person who is denied this possibility. There are many reasons for this bitterness.

First, many communities are only now recuperating from a former Jansenistic exaggeration with regard to personal talent. According to this view, the development of any talent was undesirable in itself. As a reaction against this sickly type of asceticism, some persons are now inclined to claim that one should always be allowed to develop any talent he desires, even at the expense of the duty imposed by the community situation. A second explanation may be found in the fact that persons who live in large communities engaged in widespread operations do not feel personally the pressure of the realistic life situation as it is felt by laymen who must struggle for the maintenance of a family and conform to the requirements of a professional job. Finally, as we have already seen, celibacy implies the sacrifice of a family in which one feels sorely needed as father or mother, husband or wife, and therefore deeply affirmed by the other. Some people are not able to meet the demands of this sacrifice of exclusive personal affirmation. As a result, they hunger and thirst for recognition. One way in which they can obtain this acclaim is through the development of an unusual talent or ability. In this case, ambition is based on an unconscious need to escape one of the most difficult aspects of the sacrifice involved in celibacy.

To be sure, a diocese or religious community may be faced with exceptional cases in which a talent is so unusual that it seems unjustified to deprive the Church and humanity of its fruits. In such a case, the responsible leaders or superiors may experience a serious conflict of conscience, for they must decide what the whole of reality demands of them. Should they allow the person in question to limit his life to the private restricted objectives of his diocese or religious community, or does the common good oblige them to let this extraordinary person serve a wider realm of Church and humanity? Imagine a diocese or religious community with an Einstein, Mozart, Michelangelo, a Picasso! Of course, these men are geniuses. Nevertheless, it is possible that in time to come humanity may overcome the present split between Church and culture. Outstanding cultural leaders with extraordinary gifts might then prefer the priestly or religious mode of existence to marriage or bachelorhood. Their superiors would then face a serious decision.

Besides talent, another secondary aspect of personality is the respect, and even veneration, which the true personality may arouse in those around him if they are open to the values which he embodies in his life. If he is also talented and feels it a duty to develop his abilities, he may gain wide acclaim, especially if his accomplishments appeal to his contemporaries. It is clear that the fame and the popularity of such a person are only the flower of his faithfulness to himself and to his life situation. Because he listens to the voice of Being, he fulfills himself in response to the claims of reality. And because of his motivation, he may impress receptive people very deeply, for he has obeyed the inspiration of the Spirit, telling him not to choose the broad and easy way but the narrow and exhausting one which leads to the mountain top.

In short, popularity and acclaim are only secondary gains, never to be confused with the essence of personality. This confusion is prevalent in today's world. If you ask the average man what a personality is, he will enumerate secondary, external, and striking characteristics which may be mere accompaniments to personality. He will tell you that someone is a personality when he talks and acts in a poised and easy way, when he is handsome, has a pleasant voice, and knows how to charm people with clever stories and witty quips. A personality is thus the man who can make himself the center of the crowd, get his picture in the newspapers, or appear wise and dignified while in fact he may be empty as a person.

The danger of such a reversal of primary and secondary qualities is that people make it almost impossible for themselves ever to become real personalities because they begin to strive after secondary, accidental, peripheral manifestations of being a real person. They become preoccupied with appearances. Their whole life may be concentrated on the adornment of empty shells.

Real personality, however, is existential. It is primarily self-forgetting in standing-out toward God, people, and the world. Only in turning to what one is not yet does one become a real person. One who is preoccupied with becoming a personality in a secondary sense may not even become a decent human being in the primary sense. This is even more profoundly true of the religious personality, for the religious person who concentrates on the secondary qualities of being religious is lost to religion. If he is concerned about "looking" religious, making a pious impression, behaving in an edifying manner, being praised by others for his spiritual life, then he is concentrating on the secondary characteristics of religious personality at the expense of the primary ones. He is inclined to forego an act of charity to the neighbor if this would interfere with an outward manifestation of piety. Such a person is most upset when he discovers that a superior does not think highly of his spiritual life.

We should not confuse primary or secondary personality with character and temperament. Character occupies a place between primary and secondary personality. Because it is very near to personality in the primary sense, the distinction between the two is rather subtle. Personality indicates the over-all movement of a person's differentiating and integrating existence. This movement is partly known and partly unknown to the person concerned. For the outsider, it is difficult to appraise this existential movement which the personality is. As a result of this movement certain traits are, as it were, sedimented in the attitudes and behavior of the person. Just as the movement of the glaciers millennia ago left its trace in the earth for the thoughtful observer, so the movement of existence leaves its marks on the behavior of the person. Such attitudes, behavior, and customs, which at a given moment in a life are the result of the movement which the personality is, can be called character. They are the inscriptions, the etchings, of the personality. For this reason, character can not be found in children. It takes time for existence to etch its mark on the attitudes and behavior of a person. This totality of customs and habits which we have reached at a certain moment of our life should also not be confused with secondary personality. As we have seen, the secondary traits of personality are the external and peripheral fruits of a real personal life or the cheap imitations of such manifestations in other real personalities. Not being able to be a personality himself, a person may try to mimic the smile, the posture, the voice, and the words of the real personality. In this way he may attempt to steal the external glory of accomplishment without losing his time and energy in accomplishing something himself. It is easier to look good than to be good, to sound learned than to be learned, to tell how to administer well than to administer.

Character is something deeper. It is the totality of attitudes and habits that is the result of primary personality, and its movement may underly the outward manifestation of personality in the secondary sense. For example, the late Pope John XXIII was inspired by a movement of love toward all men, whom he experienced as his brothers. This was part of his personality in the primary sense. This existential movement led in the current of his life to certain traits of character, such as his informality with people in all walks of life, of every creed and culture. As a result, certain secondary personality traits developed. He was hailed by many as an admirable, warm, and attractive person. It is easy to see that this popularity was rooted in the prime movement of his existence as observable and as embodied in certain character traits. Character is what you have; primary personality is what you are and what makes you have character; secondary personality is the result of the character that you have.

From these three we should distinguish temperament, which is quite different from all of them. Temperament is rooted in our biological make-up. It is the result of physiological factors such as our hormonal glands and our nervous system. It does not determine the existential orientation of our lives. Temperament does determine, however, the more quantitative aspects of our lives, such as the rhythm of our existence, the swiftness or slowness of our speech and movements, the optimal and minimal limits of speed within which our thought processes operate most efficiently, the intensity of our feelings, affections, and passions. The personality himself decides what is to be done with this natural rhythm, with the intensity of his passion, with the speed of his thought, but he cannot change in an absolute way the rhythm, intensity, or speed itself—at least not beyond certain limits. If he attempts to do so, he becomes awkward, tense, ineffectual, and even unhappy. A very slow person should attempt to overcome his handicap to a certain degree. However, he should realize that, since he is slow by temperament, he will never become a speedy person. If he tries to do so, he will only produce a lack of balance in his actions. A religious person who is by temperament calm or phlegmatic should never attempt to imitate, for example, the passionate exuberance of a Spanish mystic. Indeed, the confusion of temperament with religious personality could be fatal to one's development. In the grip of this misconception, one might be inclined to consider a certain slowness of movement, a certain serious dignity and quiet speech, or a certain passionate expression of religious fervor as essential to saintliness. In such a case, one would render it impossible for oneself to reach personal sanctity because holiness is to be wholly oneself in and for God.

ATTITUDE TOWARD THE ATTAINMENT OF PERFECT RELIGIOUS PERSONALITY

Another barrier to the attainment of true personality is that its splendor and attraction may lead one to an imaginary identification with the ideal. For example, a man might feel as if he is already a personality because he can speak or write about it. He imagines that he is already living on this high level because he is so responsive and elated when he reads about it. When he hears someone speak in brilliant terms of the good life on the serene heights, he feels lifted up beyond the common run of men who are not capable of sharing his noble emotions. The truth is that he only imagines himself to be a real personality. And concomitant with his elation of feeling, there may be in him a subtle repression of the awareness of his unauthenticity, imperfection, and egoism. He may forget that he must travel a long and painful road before the death of the old, immature man that is in him and the birth of the new man in Christ. In short, his thought and reading about personality or maturity, instead of helping him to grow, may have the opposite effect. It may lead him to build up in his fantasy an idealized self corresponding to the ideal of which he has read. He may then fall in love with this idealized picture. He may be so fascinated by it that he loses contact with what he really is, with his real self.

The religious person who is caught in the trap of an idealized existence reads voraciously the books written by the great mystical authors. He readily devours volumes on the various stages of the spiritual life, dwelling chiefly on the mystical state. He is elated, set afire by the sublime expressions of the saints. He is aglow with noble feelings, and it does not take long before he discovers in himself the signs that he himself is entering the paradise of which he reads. In the meantime, he ignores his real weaknesses, his hidden self-complacency. Therefore, he does not realize that his striving for the heights is tinged by the need to excel, to be better than the next person, to be the exceptional companion of the few who dwell on the peaks of highest contemplation. In a subtle way, a parallel development takes place in his relationship with other people. Before he realizes it, he looks down on them as poor inferiors engaged in the lowly housecleaning that goes on in the basement of spiritual existence. Once he is caught in this illusion, his idealized self, or dream personality, embarks on an existence all its own. Unchecked, it develops rapidly and leads to his alienation from what he really is. Others are surprised at the inconsistency between his beautiful ideals, expressions, and manners and the glaring imperfections, hidden pride, and repressed insecurity which come to the fore at unguarded moments.

For example, it is sad to observe certain public figures who have built up a popular image which is alienated from their true selves. Sometimes their need for recognition, status, and material gains is in startling contrast to the admirable picture which they present to the public. When the person who has fostered an idealized self-image suddenly receives the grace of truth concerning himself, he is visibly shaken. He tumbles, as it were, from dreamland into the realm of harsh reality. He is like a traveler who returns home from a long journey and finds his garden untended, covered with weeds, and robbed of its flowers. The very sight of it is so desolate that he doubts whether he will find the courage to start all over again to cultivate it in great labor. He is tempted to start on another journey to the land of his dreams where he will not have to work, but can admire the beautiful castles built long ago by amiable strangers. He will avoid this pitfall only if he admits to himself in humility that he still has a long way to go to become a true personality. Another temptation when faced with a fascinating ideal is to try to achieve too much in too little time. The dreamer would like to be perfect at once. He feels discouraged when he realizes that his goal will require a lifetime. He tries to skip phases of development toward it. As a result, he may end in discouragement, having a cynical attitude in respect to all ideals. Then he may even refuse to go on and proudly call his betrayal common sense and realism.

All these attitudes are basically wrong and harmful. God does not ask a person to be perfect at once. He does not even demand that he reach this summit of richness and integration at the end of his life. It may very well be that there have been events in his life, such as traumatic experiences in his childhood, that make it forever impossible for him to reach the serenity, peace, and balance of a fully integrated personality. His personal history may have burdened him with sinful inclinations which he can never eradicate. He may have deeply rooted neurotic tendencies that are incurable without psychotherapy, which he may never receive. The Lord will never ask him, "Did you reach the fullness of personality?" What counts for the Lord is the good will of man. His sanctity is dependent not on his becoming a personality but on his willing God's will. His love for Him in spite of his failure binds him more deeply to Him than his success. To be sure, if there are not too many obstacles in his natural disposition and in the history of his childhood, then grace, good will, and love for God will lead him to the fullness of personality. But even then he should be constantly aware that his demonic self never leaves him, that he retains not only love but also egocentric desire until the end of his life. Even the brightness of saintly existence is dimmed somewhat by the greyness of self-centeredness.

As we have said, what counts for God is the will. Therefore, a person with a fortunate life history may reach personal maturity even though he loves God less than his neighbor who, chained by his past history, will never reach maturity in spite of his tremendous love for the Lord. The latter may be able to avoid repeated falls through all the love and good will which he can develop with the grace of God. It may very well be that his existence, which is a failure in the eyes of men, delights the eyes of God who probes the heart of man. He may be a real saint unknown to man, known only by God. For this reason, we shall speak at length in the next chapter on man's existential will. Meanwhile, we believe that it has been profitable to consider what the full personality of man can be if grace and nature bless him with the opportunity to become a real person. It is important to know where grace and nature may lead him if both have full and free play in him from childhood on. Although it is true that a frustrated existence cannot always be made responsible for its failure and may indeed be saintly in its core, it is also true that we cannot propose such a person as a model to others. He may be an excellent example of good will, but he is a poor example of what God can reveal in a person less hampered by his past. A good insight into the characteristics of a real personality, therefore, will help superiors to appoint the right persons to the right places. Moreover, when we know the characteristics of person, we have some guidelines for our own development. We may avoid traveling toward dead ends. Finally, the vision of the ideal keeps us humbly aware of what we are not yet and may perhaps never be. It will at least inspire us to realize in small measure the appealing existence of the true personality.

DEVELOPMENT
of the Religious Personality

$$3$$

FROM WHAT we have said concerning religion and personality, it has become increasingly clear that the center of existence is the freedom of man. The only ground in which personality can grow is freedom. Unlike man, animals do not have a personality. No one speaks seriously of the personality of an elephant, a flea, or a canary, for where there is no freedom, there is no possibility to decide on a unique project of existence and to realize that project in life. In this last statement we may distinguish two movements of existence. One is to commit oneself wholeheartedly to a project. The other is the execution or the realization of that project. The two are not the same, and the first does not necessarily imply the successful fulfillment of the second. A person can be truly committed to an ideal and still be unable to make this ideal a reality in his daily life. For example, he may decide to develop a life of prayer, but it may require many years before he overcomes the obstacles which make it difficult for him to maintain the recollection necessary for a prayerful existence. In other words, he can really will something and decide for it in freedom while he is at the same time unable to do it in reality. This distinction, to which we shall return later, implies already that willing or not willing is not so simple an issue as we may have thought. Indeed, a misunderstanding of freedom, will, and decision may lead to serious complications in our religious life.

Imagine, for example, that the person who is not yet able to realize in daily life his sincere will to be a man of prayer has the mistaken notion that his failure proves that he really does not will this good, that he is a man of ill will and evil mind. In such a case, he may become discouraged even to the point of desperation. He may imagine that he is not growing in the love of God because he does not immediately succeed in the implementation of his good will in daily behavior, and as a result he may feel at odds with God. In reality, however, his sincere will and his repeated attempts to develop a life of prayer cause him to grow daily in divine love, perhaps even more so than if he had been successful, because his lack of observable results compels him to reaffirm over and over again his commitment to God, his love for God, his trust in God.

When we consider the many ways in which religious persons may misunderstand the nature and the task of the will in their religious growth, we realize that they usually err in one of two extremes which we may call *willfulness* and *will-lessness*. First we shall discuss these two one-sided exaggerations. Then we shall consider the true nature and function of the will in our existence. To distinguish the wholesome conception of our willing from the mistaken notions mentioned above, we shall call the former *existential will*.

WILLFULNESS

Willfulness emerges in man when he loses the experience of his unity. He separates his will, as it were, from other elements of his personality, such as his past history, his inclinations and passions, his imagination, his anxiety, and the power of his habits and customs. For example, a person who has never seriously studied in his life may decide to become a scholar. He foolishly thinks that if he only wills it, he can do it. So he closes himself up in his room with a stack of books and forces himself at once to study eight hours a day. After one week of this sudden change of life he may experience a breakdown. Why? Because his will is not an isolated ruler which need not take into account the other aspects of his life. In this case, the will must defer to the fact that a person who has never studied before has developed a set of physical, psychological, and emotional attitudes, customs, and habits that cannot be broken at once. They can only be changed gradually.

The will has, as it were, to sit down and start a conversation with all the other aspects, both inside and outside, which are involved in this change. If the will does not do so, it runs headlong into trouble. Of course, this is metaphorical language. In reality, my will is not an isolated thing in me, or a little person in me, which can sit down and have a conversation with other little persons. We may state the matter more explicitly: I-as-willing must take into account all the aspects which are involved in the change which I wish to make in my life. I-as-willing should not set myself apart from I-as-feeling, I-as-thinking, I-as-imagining, I-as-remembering, I-as participant-in-my-social-milieu, I-as-passionate, I-as-weak-and-sinful, and I-as-looking-toward-the-future.

For example, if I enter a postulancy or novitiate, I enter not only as a person willing to be a religious, but as a feeling, remembering, and thinking person who is willing to become a religious. In other words, I cannot cast aside all my past feelings, emotions, memories, and inclinations when I pass the threshold of postulancy or novitiate. As a beginner in the religious life, I am not reduced to a mere willing person; I am a willing person who carries with him his past. Therefore, I cannot will something as if I had no life history, interest, or feeling which I may have to overcome. To deny this would be foolish, for I would deny the reality which I am. I would be outside of my reality, and therefore I would build on unreality.

Suppose I decide that, as a future religious, I shall not be emotionally overinvolved with my family. This is a worthwhile orientation of my new existence, a necessary beginning of a life that will gradually, in the current of many years, become a life for God alone. However, this decision cannot be implemented all at once. Why?

Because the willing person which I am, in this case the person who is willing to detach himself from his family, is the same person who is still bound very closely to his family by tender feelings, living memories, and shared customs which made him part of the family until the moment of his entrance into postulancy or novitiate. He is the whole me, the real me. I cannot deny any part of him. Whether I like it or not, I shall be overwhelmed at times by my memories. In spite of the fact that I desire to live for the Lord alone, I may at times weep quietly and alone because I miss my family so much. I cannot force these feelings from me. I should not even try to do so.

On the other hand, I should not deliberately foster them or over-indulge in them. They should be an occasion for the renewal of my decision to belong to my Lord alone. I should realize that I am still very much attached to my family, but that I am also ready to grow gradually in detachment if the Lord permits me to do so. I may also discover in time what type of thought and imagination is apt to distract me from my new life and immerse me in my past existence at home. I may likewise become aware that certain occasions are conducive to my dreaming of the past. For example, I may discover that when I am not seriously occupied with my daily tasks or do not really participate in recreation, I succumb more easily to thoughts of the past which I idealize as a little paradise of pleasant company. After a long time, I may even realize for the first time in my life how people are inclined to enhance the attractive features of a past situation and to forget about the unpleasant aspects, such as quarrels, disorder, and lack of religious refinement.

It is clear from this example that the interaction of the willing me with all the aspects of my existence leads to a real growth in wisdom, makes me aware of all kinds of possibilities in myself which I never thought of. In this way I learn more from my own experience than I could ever learn from a textbook or a lecture. I become really at home with myself; I learn how to deal with myself. And because all these aspects are part of me and are precisely the same in no one else, nobody else can really teach me how to solve my problem. There are no easy and fast solutions for the problems of human growth, no solutions that can be handed to me like a medical prescription by a kind superior, and which I can execute at once. Even if such a prescription were possible, I should lose rather than gain from it, for it would rob me of the precious experience of growing insight in the midst of painful crosses.

In the case cited above, what would happen if I refused to recognize my ties to my family which were still overwhelmingly strong? These feelings would not indeed be absent. I would willfully repress the awareness of what I am; I would refuse to take into account all the aspects of my own reality. In short, I would willfully behave as if I did not have such feelings, and my life would be untrue and artificial. Moreover, I would use a tremendous amount of energy to fight off the awareness of my true self. I would have to cut off increasingly all thoughts, feelings, and perceptions which would bring back to my awareness what I refuse to recognize as being me.

When I repress my true feelings, I am not only artificial but I also become rigid, tense, and strained. My life becomes a lie; my make-believe detachment and perfection become a shining paper palace over a dormant volcano. All the feelings, passions, and memories which I refuse to recognize and to take into account are building up within the dormant volcano which I am. I become exhausted from crushing them, and at an unexpected moment later in life the volcano which I am erupts; the paper palace of my willful artificial perfection disappears in fire and smoke. This is true not only of my feelings toward home but also of all my other feelings, passions, and emotions. It is true of my sexual feelings, my envy, my jealousy, my aversion for silence and for certain types of work, my impulsive hostility toward certain persons, and my desire on a beautiful day to break away and have a wonderful time with my old friends.

Thus, I may be said to be willful when I refuse to take into account all the aspects of my life. When I do so, I try to mold my life magically. I behave like an absolute king who regards neither past nor future nor "irrational" feelings, drives, and passions. I attempt to manipulate myself into religious perfection. I deal with myself not as with a sensitive, vulnerable person but as with an inert piece of rock from which I try to fashion with heavy hammer blows the image of the perfect religious person. Such a highhanded approach to sanctity leaves me oblivious of the unconscious anxiety, bodily drives, resentments, hostile inclinations, and secret ambitions which poison my saintly motives, because the stone which I am sculpturing is not inert, without past and passion, without egocentric resistance to the chisel of the sculptor. My nature is a lively existence that moves and grows under the changes that are imposed on its surface. Imagine the amazement of a sculptor who would discover that within his statue of a madonna, a totally different image had developed, for instance, that of a devil. How disconcerted he would be if suddenly the subtle, refined, and beautiful lines of his madonna would fall apart, and the grinning face of a demon would appear to tell him, "While you were thinking that the center of this stone was inert and lifeless so that you would have to occupy yourself only with changing the surface, I have had the chance to grow wildly inside." This represents what happens to me when I try to mold and manipulate my life as a *thing* with the chisel or hammer of will power.

Superficially speaking, I may seem successful because I alter rapidly and effectively the surface of my existence, the exterior layer that covers my personality, the thin shell of my soul. However, I do not interact with the deeper layers of my existence. My life becomes regular and religious at the surface. In reality, it is a life of pious self-deceit. I can maintain it only by compulsion, for my spontaneous inner life is cut off from this peripheral religious existence. The willful me is thus closed, cumbersome, tyrannical, and compulsive. I isolate myself increasingly from my own source of vitality and spontaneity. Soon my religious existence is marked by an obstinate, stubborn, frozen mentality. My life suggests withered, dead leaves in the fall. It is as if I nailed the green wood of my life into a straight and heavy coffin. My religious existence gives people the sensation of death, of tombstones and cemeteries. Thus, "religion" often comes to be considered incompatible with the vigorous joy of living.

Moreover, when I am strained, willful, and noisily busy about my holiness, I am unable to listen to either the egocentric rumblings within me or the silent voice of grace in the core of my being. I lose my sensitivity to this voice. Nor can I listen quietly to the subtle message of the situation in which I live. My willfulness chains me to only one thing, my idealized self-image of religious perfection which I must maintain against the disturbing demands inside and outside my being. Gradually the unique aspects of my life situation, of my inner moods, and of the subtle intimations of grace are unable to communicate themselves to me at all. I have cut off all bridges between my willful striving for a perfect religious surface and the living reality of nature, grace, and my life situation. Because I no longer listen to the voice of the changing situation, I fail to recognize its uniqueness and the new response which I should create to the ever new challenge of my life history. Therefore, I must invent a pious code of stilted, identical reactions which I have readily available for every situation that may arise. I become a will-power Christian. Instead of being bound to the appeal of God in the unique reality which comes to meet me, I become addicted to my blueprint of perfect external behavior, uninspired, rigid, and precise. I assume a compulsive instead of a dialectic attitude toward my existence. Compulsive comment replaces respectful dialogue. I become a religious engineer who manipulates all objectivated "things" in my life and situation as if they were parts of an electronic computer. I become a would-be holy man. I am so busy engineering my devotional existence that no awareness remains for the sacred dimension of reality, the veiled presence of the Lord as it reveals itself through the relaxed openness of faith.

As a will-power Christian I may even develop a split or schizoid religious existence in which an isolated "higher and holier" self represses, compels, and manipulates all my human behavior without regard for reality. If such a sickness spreads among Christians, it may even give rise to a disembodied, suspended style of Christianity which is foreign to contemporary life by its refusal to be present to it. The willful Christian who is out of tune with the contemporary situation makes it impossible for Christ to incarnate Himself through him in humanity.

Another complication makes the situation more dangerous. Out of touch with myself and with reality, I, the will-power Christian, construct an idealized image not only of myself but of other people and the world. After disregarding my own reality and forcing upon myself an image of religious perfection like a rigid, wooden mask that distorts my own human face, I now feel compelled to do the same to others. My inability to listen to what others really are and to what their situation really is leads me to distort reality and to force it into the same superficial religious mold as my own life. I am tempted to overpower and willfully transform reality in others. At the moment that I as the willful Christian yield to this temptation, Christ dies in my behavior; there is born instead a fanatical, self-righteous style of faith which averts people from the good tidings that the believer claims to represent.

We may now summarize how willfulness may be discerned. When I am willful I become, first of all, closed to reality as it reveals itself to my fresh and naive perception. Instead, I develop a code of stilted perceptions of God, other people, and myself. As a result, I am unable to respond creatively to the real meaning of my situation. Instead of responding, I react blindly in a stereotyped manner. These stereotyped reactions are not real responses to the situation. They merely conform to my standardized code of perception which discloses reality not as it really is but as I should like it to be according to my willful blueprint of life and reality.

WILL-LESSNESS

The willful Christian has developed a self-image of perfect control. Basically he does not admit his weaknesses and limitations. He lives in the illusion that he can do anything if he only wills hard enough. The tragic result is that he fails to understand the deepest meaning of Christianity: the need for redemption as expressed in Scripture, dogma, and liturgy. Revelation does not stress the vain building of a perfect personality but the need for grace. It speaks little of the will power of man, but much of his weakness and sinfulness which permeates his life and even his religious motivation. The peace promised to the faithful man is rooted in the awareness of his redemption, not of his perfection. The faithful man knows that his Redeemer lives.

Therefore, I should be aware of the limitations of my will. I should not think that I can willfully build my religious existence without interaction with grace, nature, and life situations. I should not imagine that my will is all-powerful and can direct my life in splendid isolation. On the other hand, while admitting the influence of other aspects of my life, I should not exaggerate these either. I should not declare, for example, that I am so weak and limited that I can do virtually nothing, that my passions and the influence of my past are stronger than I am. Nor should I claim that grace should do all for me because I am too weak and evil to cooperate with grace in any significant way. In both cases I fall from my imaginary absolute will power to an equally imaginary lack of will. I fall from willfulness into will-lessness.

This extreme, too, is harmful to health and holiness. I now experience myself as driven either by society or by my bodily chemistry and unconscious inclinations on which I drift like a raft in a stormy sea. Such an attitude undermines my vital acceptance of initiative, guilt, and responsibility. As a result of will-lessness, my life loses spirit and inspiration; my religious existence becomes a robot Christian unable to take a personal stand in regard to my own existence. Thus I lose my ability for individual decision and for a truly personal encounter with the Lord.

When I stress too much the weakness and limitation of my will, I may develop the tendency to search for events in my life history which I can blame for my sin, failure, and imperfection. I do this to unburden myself of anxiety and guilt feelings with which I must live when I accept personal responsibility. When I believe that I am merely a puppet moved by the strings of unknown influences from my past, I escape from the experience of personal responsibility, guilt, and anxiety. I may be pleased to be without personal responsibility, like a tiny toy carried by the stream of my surroundings, for I may be unwilling to face the conflict and dialogue which will emerge when I commit myself freely to my life situation.

From the first moment of my life, my freedom is never my full possession. I must maintain it continually, and I shall always remain in danger of losing it to my impulses or to the impersonal crowd. My will is never an absolute sovereign who passes disdainfully by his bowing subjects. My will is rather a constitutional monarch who requires a diplomatic dialogue with the representatives of his unruly population in order to maintain his reign. When I am will-less and unfree, my life is defined by public opinion, social acclaim, my own impulses and passions. I love the ability to respond freely to present and past influences which I have internalized. I do not respond; I react.

When I personally appraise and evaluate a situation and discover the features that are true of this situation and no other, I may be said to be responding. Then I create from my own richness and wisdom the behavior which is most effective for me in this unique situation. When I merely react, on the other hand, I do not think personally and deeply. I do not distance myself from the situation. I do not create an interval between the stimulus and the behavior elicited by this stimulus. I act at once in an impulsive, thoughtless manner. Such a reaction is usually determined by stereotyped customs of the past or by the ways of the impersonal crowd.

For example, someone makes a cutting remark which upsets me. If I really *respond* to this remark, I am not impulsive. I attempt to calm myself, to distance myself from the first impact of the insult. I weigh the aspects of the situation. What made the person so angry with me? Perhaps he was tired, disappointed, had a bad day. Maybe I irritated him. Perhaps I was unwillingly overbearing. Would it really be wise to answer him impulsively, or would it be better to let the matter pass? Maybe I should wait and speak to him later when he feels less irritated. As a result of all these questions, I gain insight into this special person and situation. Finally, out of the richness of my thought, feeling, and past experience, I may grow to a wise response. When I *react*, however, I do not distance myself from the situation. I do not calm my agitation. Before I think, "I let him have it." One cutting remark elicits another, so that soon we insult and humiliate each other deeply. Later I am embarrassed over my unreasonable reaction.

If I am will-less and at the mercy of my impulses, I should not lose heart. No matter how weak I am, there is always a possibility in me of taking some inner stand which will transmute my mere reaction into a response. Every time I do so, my responsibility or ability to respond will expand itself and grow in strength. To be sure, I may find myself in a situation which seems for the moment unchangeable. For example, I may be so overwhelmed by jealousy that it is almost impossible for me to hide this from the other. However, this does not mean that all my freedom is gone. I can always take some stand, at least in the depth of my existence. This stand may be insignificant; it may have no immediate impact on my behavior or feelings, but it will still make a difference in my life. Simply the fact that I do not want to be jealous, even though I feel devoured by envy, already implies my taking a stand in respect to this emotion. At this moment, I already begin a dialogue between my freedom and my mood. This free decision, without having immediate effect on my envy, is nevertheless growth in holiness, magnificent commitment to God, a fresh beginning in spiritual life.

Indeed, such growth in inner holiness is sometimes more genuine, honest, and radical because it is not easily poisoned by the heady wine of successful behavior which makes me look well in the eyes of those around me. This may well be the reason why the Lord allowed certain irritating characteristics to remain in His saints. For example, St. Ignatius of Loyola was petulant and unpleasant shortly before the end of his life when a brother disturbed his nap in the afternoon. We all know saintly persons who, in spite of their best efforts, cannot overcome certain humiliating imperfections. Perhaps this impossibility is God's greatest gift to them and protects their humility. In the meantime, they grow inwardly to saintliness because they must take a stand again and again, a stand in which they reaffirm their deep inner rejection of the bad behavior which they cannot outwardly control.

We may now summarize what will-lessness means in our lives. When I am will-less, I am subservient in an impersonal way to my own impulses or to the opinions of others. I refuse to be personally open to all the meanings of reality which will reveal themselves to me only if I distance myself from my situation. This subservience leads to behavior that is either impulsive or in blind conformity to the opinions of others. The will-less person does not take into account the various meanings of his situation.

WILL, SIN, NEUROSIS, AND ORGANIC ILLNESS

We have seen that the will is always able to take a stand even if the situation is physically or psychologically unchangeable for the moment. This is also true on the boundary situations of sin and neurosis. When I am the victim of a habitual sin or of a neurosis, then my freedom and responsibility are diminished. However, I should not underestimate the responsibility which remains to me in spite of the fact that I cannot at once escape my neurotic or sinful reactions. It is the acceptance of this last shred of responsibility which can save me when I am moved by grace.

If I desire to survive spiritually, there is only one way, namely, not to identify myself with my sinful or neurotic habit, but to assume some attitude against it whenever and to the degree that I am still able to do so. It is necessary for me to maintain some areas of freedom of thought and activity, however insignificant and seemingly ineffective, against the onslaught of passion, habit, and neurosis. I must hold on to this last possibility of "not totally consenting interiorly" to that which seems to draw me in without the possibility of resistance. This preservation of a conviction of freedom, even if it does not help me to transcend totally the symptoms of neurosis and sin, will at least preserve my awareness of a last vestige of that human dignity which extends as far as freedom does. Without this awareness, everything seems lost. It is in this last outpost and refuge of my disturbed existence that grace may move me to turn to God in a dialogue between humble contrition and infinite mercy. *The Power and the Glory*, a novel by Graham Greene which reports the dialogue between the weak will of a priest and his Lord, is representative of such a boundary situation which tomorrow may be mine.

Perhaps I cannot change immediately the overwhelming impact of compulsion or passion. However, I can become aware that I am the one who suffers this weakness, that I, deep down, do not consent to it unconditionally. Then I have already overcome in part my sinful situation. My willingness to face my habitual sin and neurosis is already an act of freedom. To some extent it liberates me from despair. It is this last shred of will that counts, even though it does not lead immediately to ultimate victory.

Unenlightened pity for myself or others may incline me to deny guilt or responsibility in order to relieve anxiety. To be sure, I should strive to be free from *neurotic* anxiety which blocks my awareness of reality. But I should not willfully diminish my spontaneous experience of *normal* anxiety which emerges in every human being when faced with responsibility for his life and actions. If I do so, I may have to pay for this relief with the false conviction that I am essentially a moral cripple without the possibility of taking a human stand in the area of my affliction. In this case, instead of having a neurotic or sinful habit, I become this habit. I immerse myself in it. I identify with it, just as a sick animal is one with its illness and unable to assume an attitude toward it.

Moreover, my repression of normal guilt and anxiety will lead to neurotic guilt and anxiety. To accept free will means to accept responsibility and to bear it. I should not renounce my last shred of potential freedom. On the contrary, I should make it the center of renewal. I should accept, face, and explore my unconscious drives, passions, past sins, and the influence of the sensual civilization which I have unwittingly internalized.

My awareness of sinfulness will keep alive the awareness of my need for redemption. When I unveil the base realities in my life, I orient myself as a willing, searching Christian. I am already engaged in the assumption of a religious stand, in some exercise of freedom, in some acceptance of responsibility. I am already breaking the bond of impulse, passion, and past experience by going beyond it in conscious and courageous exploration. My growing awareness of these deterministic influences in my existence will liberate me increasingly from their dominance.

Today we find an increasing number of psychologists and psychiatrists who realize the primacy of the spiritual or, as they prefer to call it, the primacy of the existential over the organismic, the instinctual, and the environmental. When one attends the meetings of Alcoholics Anonymous or of Recovery Incorporated, one becomes aware how this appreciation of man's existential resiliency has been implemented in certain modes of group therapy. The members of these groups humbly admit the presence of dark impulses. At the same time they recount the ways in which they were able to transcend them, and thus encourage one another to cope spiritually with psychological negativity. Many of these people impress one by a peace and serenity which seem the more tangible because they are maintained in the face of tremendous odds.

It is true that my behavior is conditioned, but I can influence the kind of conditioning by the meaning which I freely impose on my tendencies and my environment. For example, when I perceive my father, teacher, boss, or superior as an authoritarian guardian who watches my movements in order to inhibit my growth and spontaneity, my behavior will be conditioned by that perception. In the presence of my superior, I shall behave as an anxious and subdued, or as a rebellious and aggressive, person. On the other hand, when I perceive my superior not only as a person with authority but also as a human being who is able to understand me to some degree, my behavior will be conditioned to this image. I shall be more at ease, relaxed, and spontaneous in his company. An interesting result is that, in the latter case, I shall be less and less able to speak of conditioning my behavior in the strict sense. As we have seen, the more relaxed, spontaneous, and open I am, the more I grow to unique responses which are newly created, at least in part, by this free spontaneity.

Similarly, when I suffer from sinful or neurotic habits, I bear a degree of responsibility for the meanings which I uncover in these predispositions. For example, I can freely decide that my bad habit means that I cannot do anything about it. In this case, I surrender; my behavior will be conditioned by the deterministic meaning which I have imposed on my sin or neurosis. Or I can freely decide that my sin or neurosis is a challenge, an occasion for growth in humility and self-understanding, a repeated opportunity for reaffirmation of my basic commitment to God. In this case, my behavior will develop in the light of this freely chosen meaning. It may be that I shall never be rid of my sin or neurosis, but my repeated stand may help me to grow to the summit of holiness, to profound understanding of the human predicament as dramatized in my constant struggle, and to merciful and tender love for fellow men who suffer as I do from sin and neurosis.

As we have seen, I can always find a free inner orientation in situations which I cannot immediately change. Is this also true of organic illness? A striking example can be found in the life of the Venerable Francis Libermann. He was a convert from Judaism who revitalized the educational Society of the Holy Ghost Fathers and expanded its originally exclusive dedication to higher education so that the congregation would consist not only of professors but also of members dedicated to elementary and secondary education and to the care of souls in parishes and in missionary countries. The Venerable Libermann suffered from epilepsy, which postponed his ordination to the priesthood for ten years. He experienced such strong tendencies toward suicide that in self-protection he had to remove all sharp objects from his room. Many experts have written on epilepsy and its physiological and psychological manifestations. When we compare their descriptions with the accounts of Libermann's behavior as given by the witnesses to his attacks, we are

aware of a strong difference between the serene response of Libermann and the reactions described by neurologists.

Traditional psychology and psychiatry are pervaded by social and
biological determinism. They underestimate the distinction between
a patient's spontaneous inclinations, which are linked with his
physio-psychological disturbance, and the stand which his deepest
self may assume when he faces, accepts, and explores his inclinations. In principle, the ultimate attitudes of an epileptic can be
molded more by what his propensities mean to him than by the
predispositions themselves. We see in Libermann a spontaneous
inclination to suicidal depression, isolation, and feelings of inferior-
ity. But his will, the core of his suffering existence, transcended inclinations which he was unable to dismiss. When the option of the
spirit transcends the inclinations which are linked with a serious
illness, then the situation becomes a stepping stone to greater maturity, deeper spirituality and, in the case of a truly religious man,
genuine sanctity. The illness becomes a blessed illness, a sacred
appeal to live more authentically; the continuous pull of depression
compels the patient to renew his spiritual option against the seduc-
tion of despair. It makes it impossible for him, moreover, to succumb
to a shallow existence, problemless, impeccable, and monotonous
as a carefully arranged cemetery. He has to choose between a de-
generating and an heroic existence. It is actually difficult for him
to be a decent, mediocre man. A similar situation may arise in the
case of other disturbances, such as invincible homosexual tendencies,
alcoholism, and nymphomania. Every new fundamental option of
such a person in the face of spiritual and moral destruction reinforces and strengthens his spiritual stand. The quality and degree
of this transcendence is dependent on the depth of his motviation.
Father Libermann's motivation had a dimension of supernatural
depth, inspired as it was by grace. Therefore, he reached an extraordinary degree of serene transcendence of the negative tendencies aroused by his illness.

EXISTENTIAL AND RELIGIOUS WILL

I can thus take some stand even in the situations of sin, neurosis,
or organic affliction. I can do so because my will has an existential

or dialectical nature. My will is not, as we have seen, the absolute ruler imagined by the will-power Christian. Nor am I the will-less product of my past, my impulses, passions, or environment. My will is my ability to respond to reality as it reveals itself to me in a situation, even when I am not able to change this reality in all its factual aspects. My ability to respond is transformed and nourished by grace. This transformation enables me to respond freely to God and to His will as They manifest Themselves in my life situation. What the Lord allows in a given situation escapes my manipulation. My life situation is a challenge, an invitation, an appeal which comes to meet me in its uniqueness. It demands my personal response. It is not of my making; rather, it makes me while I respond faithfully to its manifestations. Therefore, I-as-religiously-willing am fundamentally "openness" and "affirmation." If I am truly religious, I am open to the presence of the divine. At the same time, my life becomes increasingly an affirmation of the divine will and presence. My religious will becomes unconditional commitment and surrender to His mysterious design. In other words, I-as-religious-will am a fundamental readiness to face and affirm God's presence as it reveals itself in my daily situation.

The manifold reality which God allows to be in and around me manifests itself to me daily if I am open to its message. To be willing is to be open, whereas unwillingness is the refusal to listen to the message of reality. At every moment I can open or close myself to the intimations of God's will. When I am open I am receptive with my whole being, not only with my logical mind but also with my intuition, not only with my eyes and ears but also with my emotional sensitivity, not only with my imagination but also with my memory, for my past experience enlightens me concerning the situation of the moment.

I-as-willing am thus openness to all revelation of reality that Providence allows in my situation. This willing openness is the permanent source of the manifold moods, feelings, memories, imaginations, and perceptions which particularize, as it were, my fundamental openness. They are special modifications of my primordial openness to my situation. For example, if I decide to grow to a truly religious existence, I become increasingly a willing openness for all manifestations of the presence of God in the reality which surrounds me. This willingness to experience the Lord in my life leads to a special openness to all my modalities of existence.* When I walk in the country, I see with a new eye the beauty of trees and flowers. I see and hear with eyes and ears like those of St. Francis, whose willing openness to God gave him a fresh perception of the sun, the moon, the stars, and even the graceful animals playing in forest and stream. Moreover, my emotional modality of existence shares in this transformation. When I hear a poem or a sermon which is a moving expression of God's love, I may experience deep joy or awe; my willing openness inclines my emotions to experience God also on this level of my existence. When I must speak of God, my willing openness prompts my memory to recall the tangible marks of His presence in my past. Thus my openness guides me to recollect past knowledge and experience to meet my present need.

This is not all. The willing openness which pervades my existence grows toward a firm decision which is a response of my whole being to that which reveals itself to my openness. For example, I may be a willing openness for what God wants me to do in my life, whether it be marriage, the unmarried state in the world, the priesthood, brotherhood, or sisterhood. This willing openness makes my memory stand out toward my past in order to detect any sign of God's plan for my life. At the same time, it enhances my sensitivity and intellectual perspicacity for any manifestation of God's will in regard to my vocation. As a result, I develop probing thoughts, spontaneous feelings, perceptions, and inclinations which all in their own way tell me something of what God seems to want for me as a life vocation. I gather together, in the core of my being, all of the experience yielded by all my modalities of existence. In this inner recollection, I grow increasingly to a final decision. I come to see what my life should be according to God's will. Finally, I bring together all my

---

* Modalities of existence are the various instrumental ways in which man can stand out into reality such as intellectual, imaginative, emotional, and perceptive ways. A modality of existence is not the same as a mode of existence. A mode of existence is a fundamental over-all orientation of one's presence to the world. For example, one's fundamental over-all mode of presence to a person may be a presence in love. This attitude of love orients one's modalities of presence to the beloved such as one's thoughts, feelings, and imaginations about him.

insights within a prudent project of existence which is in harmony with God's design and revelation.

Thus I reject none of my existential modalities nor the knowledge which they give me. I do not repress nor deny their voice. I do not say to myself that this attraction or that aversion should not be taken seriously, or that I should not consider this memory of the past. On the contrary, all my feelings, all my relevant memories, all my imaginations obtain a fair hearing in the core of my existence, even if they seem initially contradictory. I do not manipulate or repress my emotionality; I discipline it. I should not understand "discipline" in the compulsive, forceful, and rationalistic sense of the punishment of a prison. Rather, I should understand it in the etymological sense of the word, referring to "disciple": My will as openness inclines all my modalities of existence to the divine presence in all things. It makes them disciples of the sacred dimension of reality. Thus, in the example given above, the recollection of past knowledge and inspiration leads to a seeing again, a hearing again, a remembering again, a feeling again, a thinking again until I, as a complete existence, become clear about what reality is telling me concerning the will of God for my life. His presence and will are veiled by daily appearances and unveiled by the eyes of faith.

When I am a will-power Christian, I subdue reality in myself and in my surroundings instead of listening in openness to divine inspiration. I do not look at what is. I have eyes only for my little blueprint of life, my willful plan of self-coercion. This will to power is out of tune with the voice of the Lord. His voice is heard, not by the powerful, but by the meek and humble of heart who possess the earth. Possessing the earth means that they are able to discover and to use earthly possibilities wisely and effectively without violating their sacred dimensions. He who tries to break reality will be broken. Such a breakdown sometimes leads to neurosis or psychosis. When my religious will is authentic, I grow increasingly toward wise and harmonious projects of existence which are in tune with the will of the Lord.

Even this is not the whole story. Authentic will leads not only to the full openness of my existence and to the decision for a project of existence; it also leads to the concrete embodiment of such a project in my daily life. This embodiment makes it necessary for me to be open to the concrete situation in which I hope to realize my decision. But this time my openness is an alertness to the practical aspects of the situation. Now it is not so much a question of making up my mind about what I should be in life, but of prudently and effectively realizing my ideal to some degree at this moment. How can I do something about it in my special environment? What would be a workable long-range plan?

As soon as I decide on a project of existence, I am faced with a never-ending series of theoretical and practical questions. These demand practical proposals which embody my theoretical existential decision. They also demand the execution of these proposals, which will require support from the will. Sometimes I am tired. At other moments I feel aversion to getting down to the task at hand. The over-all readiness of my existential will now translates itself into the thrust necessary to bring me over the hump of inner resistance or childish desire. We may call this action the functional aspect of the will. In all its concrete forms, it is secondary in nature; it is a derivative of my authentic existential will; it is a practical consequence of my primary openness. If I were totally closed in the core of my being toward a certain task or enterprise, I would not even think of theoretical plans and practical ways of executing them. All forms of theoretical and practical knowledge which help me to realize my existential project *presuppose* in me a more fundamental, willing openness. It is willing openness which permits me to see, both theoretically and practically, what I should do in my unique life situation.

The same may be said about my active execution of my plans in concrete behavior. In fact, I should seriously question my will and orientation if I almost never have theoretical or practical ideas about those things which I claim to do willingly. I should doubt my willingness even more if I frequently find it impossible to overcome the small resistance which everyone experiences in getting down to work. Another sign that there may be something ambiguous about my basic decision is the sudden appearance of nearly insurmountable resistance when I am faced with my special duty. In such cases, it is not very helpful to attack the immediate difficulty or to apply brute force to drive myself mercilessly to those tasks for which I experience a mounting aversion. It is better to explore what I really will in the depths of my existence. Perhaps I do not will what I claim to will; what I disclaim as my desire may well be a deep, unconscious but dynamic drive in my life.

For example, a young Christian intellectual may feel that his deepest willingness is to further Christianity by a splendid intellectual performance, by a life dedicated to scholarship, by the countless hours of silent and humble service at his desk. Moreover, he may hope to inspire his fellow Christian intellectuals to the same appreciation of the cultural mission of the Church. However, when he looks carefully at what he is really doing, he discovers a surprising discrepancy between his actions and his ideals. He is content as long as he can talk about his projects, especially before large audiences and admiring students. He is satisfied as long as he can hurl passionate diatribes at those Christians who supposedly do not share the scholarly devotion of the few chosen ones like himself. All goes well as he excitedly pens letters to the editor. He feels on top of the world when his picture appears in the newspapers over his daring statements to the PTA group of his parish. However, he notices one curious thing. As soon as he attempts to put all his high-sounding assertions into action, he fails miserably. He talks splendidly about the scholarly dedication of the modern Christian, but he is unable to spend many hours behind his desk daily, as scholarly non-Christians do. He declares to his adulating audience that the Christian intellectual should be present in the arena of modern thought with his own contribution. But his contribution does not amount to one publication a year. He clamors that Christian education should be reformed, should be brought up to standard. But his lectures are thin, unscholarly, directed more toward gaining adulation from excitable adolescents than instilling in them the discipline of true learning. He is enthusiastic about reforms in the liturgy, but he neglects the literature of his own field of study. He admits to himself that he experiences insurmountable resistance when he is faced with hours of intensive study behind his desk, with the solid preparation of a well-organized, original lecture for his class, with the struggle with the latest ideas in his field of competence.

Such a man may well ask himself, "Is my deepest will really to contribute to the intellectual growth of Christianity? Or is my deepest will to have my picture in the papers, to be adulated by the immature, to be the man about town, to make a name for myself, to be something very special in my own eyes and in the eyes of others?" He may discover that the latter is the drive which motivates him and which tempts him to use the propaganda for Christian scholarship as a springboard for his own aggrandizement. He may now be able, perhaps for the first time in his life, to grow to authenticity, to destroy the lie of his life, to become a sincere person not only on the conscious but also on the unconscious level of his existence. He should not be distressed by his self-discovery, which is a gift of grace, because now he has the opportunity to become a real Christian in deed, not merely in word.

To sum up, when I am a religious person my willing openness for the manifestation of God's presence in all situations is the permanent source and foundation of all my actions, judgments, and decisions and of all my theoretical and practical knowledge.

My religious will, finally, is my primordial decision and readiness to respond to the hidden voice of the Lord, to disclose the sacred dimension of reality, and to let the presence of the divine in all-that-is reveal itself. As a religious man I sanctify the universe, not by conquering it, but by guarding its sacred dimension, for reality can reveal itself to me in many ways. For example, when I look out of my window at the trees in the park, their reality can disclose itself to me in a variety of dimensions. When I look with the eyes of a carpenter, I see the trees as solid material for boards and planks which I may use in the construction of furniture and buildings. Again, I may view the same trees as a biologist. Then they reveal themselves to me as belonging to special classes of plants. This is a dimension of reality quite different from the practical dimension of the carpenter. When I am hungry, I may see the red apples on the trees in the tasty and edible dimension of their reality. In other words, the particular dimension of reality which exists in my world of thought and perception depends on the stand which I take. If no one in the world took the practical stand of the carpenter, the dimension of trees as material for building would disappear in our shared world of meaning. Even if I myself am not interested in trees as a source of usable wood, I am still reminded of this dimension by the carpenters in my society. In this sense, carpenters are the guardians of a practical dimension of trees in the universe of meaning which is my culture.

Similarly, this principle can be applied to religious existence. When a deeply religious man looks at trees in the park, he experiences the presence of the Creator in His creation, the expression of divine beauty in the splendor of green leaves and lacy boughs. He communicates this experience to others in his society, and in this sense, he is the guardian of the sacred dimension of reality. The saint is not the willful ethical superman, but the humble shepherd of the sacred. As the shepherd peacefully tends his flock and does not allow any sheep to stray, so the saintly man carefully cultivates his lively perception of divine presence in all people, things, and events in the world. He does not allow the vision of the divine to perish among mankind. Even if all those around him are attracted by only the profane appearance of reality, the saint remains the lonely shepherd of the sacred dimension of the world. He will not permit it to perish in the cold hearts of men. As long as there is one religious existence in the world, there will be at least one human being who safeguards the sacred in our world of meaning.

Although I am not a saint, I should realize that the chief meaning for mankind of my religious existence is the same as that of the saint. Therefore, as a religious person I should be present according to my talents in the realms of nature, art, science, and culture. If the religious person refuses to be present, who will rescue the sacred dimension of these realities? What shepherd will tenderly tend the flock of the divine aspects of every realm of human endeavor? As a truly religious existence, I am not primarily a man of many devotions, but the faithful guardian of the religious meaning of the world. The openness of my religious will, transformed and nourished by grace, enlightened by Revelation, gives rise constantly to the sacred dimension of reality and preserves its mysterious, tenuous presence in every situation.

We may now summarize what existential will and religious will really are. My existential will is, first of all, my personal openness to reality as it reveals itself to me. It is, second, my subsequent personal option and execution of behavior which integrates all relevant meanings of my situation. My religious will is, first, my personal openness—in the light of Revelation and under the impulse of grace —to reality as it reveals itself to me as a sanctified member of the Body of Christ. It is, second, my subsequent option and execution of behavior which incorporates all relevant meanings, sacred and profane, of my situation.

DEVELOPMENT OF AUTHENTIC RELIGIOUS WILL

If I desire to maintain and foster my religious existence, it is of primary importance to preserve my religious will, to promote its authenticity, to prevent its decline. First of all, in the relationship between will and "lived" reality, I should never replace dialogue by denial. My "lived" reality is all that I am at any moment: my good intentions, my noble feelings, but also my hostile impulses, sensual urges, and vain ambitions. I, as willing, should not deny the presence of all these modes of existence. Instead of denying them, I, as willing, should interact with them. I should never replace this dialogue by denial in the relationship between me-as-willing and me-as-lived reality.

The will-power Christian abuses his will in the negation of irrational wishes instead of facing them in the light of Revelation. Often I am not humble enough to admit the presence of base inclinations which would deflate my self-esteem. I can maintain such a denial of my "bad" impulses only by a negation of my spontaneous awareness of them. To prevent my becoming spontaneously aware of my desires, I have to curb my spontaneity more and more. This attitude may lead to a virtual extinction of my spontaneity. As a result, I live increasingly in an emotional vacuum. Unfortunately, this death of my sensitivity will also impoverish my possibility of full religious experience, for religious experience is not simply a question of acrobatics of my logical intelligence.

When I increasingly repress my spontaneity, I may sooner or later sense that something is missing in my life. Because of my repression, I cannot define what is missing, but I vaguely suspect that others possess it. As a result, I may resent their naturalness, their relaxed and spontaneous manner. I experience an obscure feeling of irritation with people who seem to exist exuberantly and "dangerously," without fear of doom and damnation. However, my self-image of achieved perfection does not allow me to admit to myself that I have this feeling of irritation. I repress my resentment and envy instead of exploring the message of these emotions in my life. If I investigate what evokes these feelings in me, I may perhaps discover that I cannot bear to see others freely enjoy what I have mutilated in my own life. This is not all. When I deny such feelings instead of facing them and working them through, they do not disappear. They come to the fore in other ways which seem more pious and apostolic and are therefore acceptable to me because they do not conflict with my self-image of religious perfection. My irritation with those who have not killed in themselves the joy of life and the beauty of spontaneity masquerades as aggressive "apostolate," "fraternal correction," "moral censorship," and "holy concern for unholy brethren."

It is clear that such hidden inclinations may spoil my pious enterprise. My repressed hostility may sabotage my apostolic motives, thus transforming my zealous apostolate into something fanatic and distasteful without my realizing it on the level of awareness. I may become a master of indictment and denunciation of fellow Christians who think and speak spontaneously and blaze new trails for Christianity. If my sickness develops, I may become a one-man inquisition; not being permitted to torture my fellow Christians on the rack, I slash them with my tongue and with my small-minded, but well-meant, insinuations. This is the tragedy of my repressed hostility, that I am unaware of it on the conscious level of my existence where I really feel like a holy defender of the Faith. This role is in keeping with the self-image of religious righteousness that I have built up by the repression of the awareness of what my real feelings are.

Spontaneity radiates richness, warmth, and charm in Christian existence and keeps it vigorous and creative. My will, therefore, should not negate spontaneous inclinations but should give them direction. The dried-up, compulsive Christian is the conceited do-gooder with only will and no spontaneity. On the other hand, the person with mere spontaneity is irresponsible, playful, and childish. As an adult he may abuse religion, as a kind of playboy Christian, for his own impulsive ends; or he may become a robot Christian moved by any wind which blows in the collectivity of people to which he blindly belongs without coming into his own personality.

If my religious existence is authentic, my will and my spontaneity are welded harmoniously. Together they lead to my prudent option of the best suitable project of action for me. Then my option ripens in the light of grace and Revelation while I listen respectfully to the spontaneous rise of inclinations which reveal the richness of possibilities in me and my situation. I do not deny nor exclude my spontaneity; I incorporate and transcend it. My wholesome growth in religious existence means that I integrate my spontaneity, will, and decision in the light of grace and Revelation.

This religious harmony is possible in me only when I am aware of my spontaneous inclinations, no matter how mean or exalted, childish or mature, hostile or loving, envious or altruistic, greedy or generous. I may feel anxiety and shame when I admit to myself my immaturity, my smugness, my jealousy and hate, for such feelings belie the elated image of my religious perfection. It is this image which has led me to repress the awareness of such demeaning inclinations in myself. The practice of a deep and genuine examination of conscience will help me to maintain this honest self-awareness which is the foundation and beginning of all growth in the spiritual life. I may need a spiritual director who is able and willing to assist me in unmasking my deceit and pretension. In the case of neurosis, psychotherapy may be necessary to remove cataracts which blur my vision. This *becoming aware* is central in the beginning of my religious life. Later I may be focused on living union with the divine presence. But even then a marginal attention to what deep down I "am inclined to be" should remain a permanent precaution against decline in religious authenticity.

It is crucial for my growth that I relate the initial awareness of my spontaneity with the awareness of myself as a responsible person. I must admit that my inclinations are my own. I have to face them and answer for them. I should not look on my inclinations as if I were an outsider, safe and withdrawn. I cannot take a vantage point outside myself from which I manipulate like an engineer all that transpires in my life. I must "own" my spontaneous experiences which reveal my reality, my situation, my world. I should experience deeply that my situation reveals itself in my feelings and inclinations as an appeal of possibilities to be realized in action.

I can respond to this appeal in a variety of ways, but I should not deny any awareness which announces itself in my lived experience. The authentic will chooses to be open to reality as it reveals itself. As soon as I open up to what is, reality reveals itself in ever-increasing detail; each particular revelation implies a challenge to respond to it in an authentic way, once I experience this aspect of reality as mine. I am the one who has these inclinations. They are appeals to me, invitations to options and actions of mine. They reveal to me a world of attractive possibilities which I can realize or not realize, totally or only partially realize. I am the person who must bind some of these inclinations to a consciously assumed project of life, while omitting others which would distort the harmony of my project.

It is my spirit which enables me to transcend my immediate situation, to assume a distance from impulse and inclination and from the attractive aspects of the world which they reveal to me. As a human spirit, I can distance myself and ponder in terms of the possible. This taking of distance is a necessary condition for the possibility of my will to assume weight in my life; hence, the necessity for asceticism, recollection, and inner moderation which, among other things, keep my ability to distance myself flexible and available at moments of confusion, crisis, and temptation.

This detachment enables me to ponder which inclinations I should foster and which ones I should pass by, without repressing my humble consciousness that it is I who have these inclinations. Then grace will enable me to decide on a religious project, which is not a denial of all inclination, but an incorporation of spontaneity on the higher level of consciousness in the light of grace and revelation. In other words, the good will of the religious person cannot blindly act on his propensities but can only live with them in a dialectical relationship. To give an example: the experience of my inclination toward an attractive person on the level of spontaneity may bring delight and the longing to continue or renew the experience; but the realization that I am the person who is experiencing this excitement and desire makes me aware of the implications which the willing affirmation, continuation, or renewal of this experience may have for my life, my relationship with God, with my marriage partner, my children, my vocation. The prudish refusal of willful piety to admit that it is I who experience this delight and longing may lead to a risky relation under false pretense of utility or concern. This bad faith veils the real inclination which is driving me on. Repressed from awareness, the excitement grows coarsely like a hidden, unchecked cancer which may overwhelm my existence. Finally it may be detected, when perhaps only traumatic surgery may be able to save the integrity of two self-deceived people and the happiness of others linked with their existence.

My option as a Christian should be a religiously responsible option. Religious responsibility involves, first, responding to my situation in the light of the Revelation of my religion; second, responding to God's unique revelation in my unique situation as it manifests itself to me in my daily life. Thus, my response to what I experience as God's personal revelation to me in my unique situation should always be in conformity with the Revelation which God has given to all mankind in and through Christ and His Church. Both responses presuppose that I see reality with the eyes of faith. It is faith which makes visible to me the dimension of the sacred. This vision of faith is a gift which cannot be forced, but which will be bestowed on me when I am ready for its intimation. The constant practice of asceticism, recollection, and inner moderation leads to an attitude of silent readiness in which the vision of faith may appeal to my existential will. Finally, in this light of faith I shall respond wisely to all the aspects of my situation. In this religiously responsible attitude, my will transcends the immediacy of impulse and inclination.

But, again, I can transcend only what I own in awareness. Therefore, it remains important, even for the deepest religious decision, that it be preceded by a dialogue with spontaneity. As a result of this dialogue, I may have to decide to do what is precisely the opposite of some of my most intense desires, while affirming other inclinations which can be ratified by my project of religious existence. Again, a serene and moderate practice of mortification will keep me ready and capable, with the grace of God, to follow up my decisions in so far as they are always necessarily opposed to some part of myself which is neither denied nor realized. In any case, I shall not bury that spontaneity which I cannot promote in my project of existence. Otherwise, I may be sabotaged by unconscious propensities which corrupt the behavior necessary to carry out my project. Neither shall I fall into the opposite extreme and willfully excite and foster the awareness of propensities which I cannot realize without distorting the harmony of my religious mode of being. Willful excitation as well as willful repression of inclinations which are irrelevant to my authentic religious project injure the peace and wholeness of my existence.

Although I should quietly examine my impulses lest they betray the consistency of my religious being-in-the-world, I must also accept the fact that I can never assess exhaustively all my inclinations under all possible aspects. Therefore, I can never be sure that my religious option or project has attained optimal purity and perfection. My humble suspicion of the taint of selfish impulse keeps alive in me the need for redemption. I shall humbly accept that my motives are not fully transparent to me because I am not a pure spirit, but a fallen human being in need of purification. I shall be satisfied with a peaceful pondering of my intentions within the limits of reason and possibility. The rest I shall leave to God in surrender. A disregard for the limits of my capacity of self-awareness will betray itself in tenseness, anxiety, compulsion, scrupulosity, and an over-all loss of serenity of heart and mind. These are symptoms of a willful purification of motive and inclination, which is a stubborn attempt of the will to act on the limits of self-awareness instead of relating to these limits dialectically. It is the refusal of my will to admit my essential imperfection, to acknowledge that I cannot plumb the depths of my sinfulness and deceit, that I cannot save myself but need redemption.

The discovery that I cannot willfully force optimal purification may hurt my pride. I may fall from willfulness into the void of will-lessness, thus refusing to be satisfied with the relative purification that I may attain with God's grace. It is this all-or-nothing attitude which defeats the possibility of a truly existential or dialectical will, and which leads to the fallacy of absolute will-power or of will-lessness. The necessary condition for the possibility of existential will is humility. Humility is the recognition of my essential limitation which implies the necessity of dialogue. When grace liberates my will from absolutism, laxity, and determinism, I may be faithful to the existential nature of my will. Then I may grow humbly and serenely to the limited perfection which Providence intended for me from all eternity. Then, I may increasingly discover God's project for me and realize it humbly in my option and action.

THE PREPARATORY PHASE OF RELIGIOUS DEVELOPMENT

We have considered religious existence from various points of view. We have seen its differentiation in various modes and modalities. A *mode* of existence is a full and integrated way of being in the world. For example, when I am present to my daily situation in a prayerful mode, all my modalities of existence participate in this mode. I see things in a different way; my emotions are easily touched by the immanence of the divine; I am interested in the word of God; I gratefully remember His gifts in the past. Even the movements of my body reveal the recollection of my heart. When I live in this prayerful mode of existence, it thus integrates all my modalities, it orders and directs them, pervades and permeates them with its special over-all orientation.

A *modality* of existence, however, does not have this integrating nature of a mode. Instead of orienting, it is oriented. Instead of integrating, it is integrated in a higher design of life. A modality of existence, such as feeling, seeing, hearing, remembering, anticipating or imagining, is instrumental. It makes my being in the world possible, for it would be impossible for me to be in the world as a prayerful mode of existence if I did not have eyes, ears, emotionality, memory, and imagination.

Thus far we have discussed both the integration and the differentiation of my religious existence. As a well-integrated religious personality, I am a person who has decided with his whole being on a religious project of life. This project integrates all my other modes of existence, which are permeated by my religious mode of being, and these integrated modes integrate in turn all my existential modalities. We have also presented an ideal picture of what religious personality would be if it were fully achieved. And we have discussed the core of religious existence, my free existential will. We have yet to consider another feature of religious development. During the long history of his growth in personality, the religious person finds himself successively on what we may call different planes or levels of existence.

My religious mode of being is a standing-out in reverence and surrender toward a Being whom I experience as the personal Transcendent, the ultimate ground of all that is and, therefore, of my own being. Being religious is a mode of existence; it is not merely a feeling, a thought, a style of behavior, or a moral code. My religious life is the very foundation of all these possible manifestations. My religious mode of being is a basic commitment of my whole existence, even when the partial and incidental manifestations of this commitment, such as religious feeling, thought, and action, are temporarily absent.

This religious mode of life is not something new or unusual. We find its appearance wherever men appear. It accompanies the history of the human race. It is expressed in the symbols of, and was a basic influence in, all cultures which men have explored. Healthy religious development has always been essential to strong cultures. Unwholesome fixations of this development, wherever they have been found, have sooner or later arrested the growth of the culture and led to psychopathology in its members.

When we consider the gradual development of the religious mode of existence in cultures or in individuals, we distinguish various levels of attainment which are reached at certain moments of their historical or individual growth. For our purpose, we shall give special attention to these levels as they appear in us as individuals.

I may distinguish three main phases of development in my religious mode of existence, namely, a preparatory phase, a phase of proper development, and an abiding, embodying phase of development.

In the beginning of my spiritual life I am in the preparatory stage of my religious growth. I have not yet found the proper object of my religious mode of existence. I may not even know what I am looking for. I may be searching for the divine without being aware of it. My deepest longing is for God but, not knowing that my desire is for Him alone, I may look for other people and other things which temporarily take the place of God for me. This striving of my whole existence for God is thus transferred to someone or something less than He is. I may call this transference of my existential desire an existential transference. As long as I am not mature enough to find God Himself, I may go through many of these existential transferences. I may become fascinated by many people and things as if they were God Himself. Therefore, we may say that the preparatory phase of religious development consists of a series of existential transferences which are due to my unconscious search for the proper object of my religious mode of existence.

I may conceive of my life as an unconscious inclination to stand outside or beyond myself, to continually surpass what I am by increasing participation in reality, in Being. My striving for deeper participation takes the form, first, of personal encounter with the people around me. Reality becomes familiar to me in and through my encounter with another person. My need for personal participation in the life of another may be conceived religiously as the restless desire of my being to ex-ist, to stand out into a personal, all-perfect, infinitely tender Being. The mystery of this Being reveals itself to me in a multiplicity of beings, but primordially and most effectively in the personal being of my fellow man, of my father, mother, brother, sister, teacher, clergyman, friend, sweetheart, husband or wife. In other words, my very being is an all-pervasive longing for the all-good, all-powerful, all-protective, that I cannot name but that attracts me steadily and keeps me in its orbit. As we have seen, however, this deepest longing of my whole existence for infinite Being can be transferred to one of its limited manifestations, such as my own ego, another human being, or attractive things, events, institutions, and cultures. In this manner, I transfer my existential yearning for participation in all-goodness, all-beauty, all-powerfulness of Being to a particular being which I invest with these pure ultimate perfections.

My existential transference is called narcissistic when it is oriented toward my own ego as the omnipotent, magic, all-good Being. When I am a small infant, it is normal for me to be narcissistic, for, then, my experiences are very limited. Most of them are centered in the needs of my organism: I feel hungry, cold, wet, sleepy, lonely, thirsty. I myself cannot do much for the relief of these needs which make me anxious and uncomfortable. Therefore, as long as I am in this helpless state, the relief of such needs is my exclusive concern and preoccupation. It seems to me that all good is in the fulfillment of these desires of my body. It is as if my whole existence is centered on myself alone, as if my innate striving for all goodness, truth, and beauty is transferred to the little manifestation of Being which I am.

When my development is normal, the deep religious striving— which I am—develops beyond this stage of existential narcissism in the search for its proper object. It may be, however, that my parents did not take loving and consistent care of the needs of my helpless body. In this case, it will be difficult for me to go beyond the narcissistic orientation of my religious drive because the absence of loving and consistent care made me overanxious. I became so concerned about my survival in a world where nobody really seemed to care about me that I cannot believe it is safe to give up my preoccupation with my own needs. I do not dare to forget myself even for a moment and to really enjoy the presence of others. As a result, the development of my religious quest is halted, is nipped in the bud; I am fixated on myself, and I may never be able to find God and the other so long as I am not sure that I can trust others.

This narcissistic fixation may poison my whole life and even my encounter with God until I find a loving person who, with infinite patience, can make up to me for what I missed as a child. Then this person, perhaps a good psychotherapist, becomes for me like John the Baptist, who was not himself the Lord but opened the way for the Lord. Such a person, however, must have great resources of love and tolerance, as I shall be inclined to relate to him as a small capricious infant relates to his mother. I may have moments in which I feel compelled to try the patience of this person in unreasonable, childish, and even mean ways. I make him suffer much because I am so distrustful of the love and care of people. I cannot believe that someone really cares and I cannot feel secure because I have never once experienced in my life that somebody else can care for me unconditionally, no matter what I do or say, regardless of my "ungoodness" and meanness. Only when I really experience that I am still accepted and not rejected, only then will I dare to go beyond myself, to leave the presence to my own ego and to develop the religious quest which I am. The other person has to enable me to live through a stage which is necessary for the development of my religious life, for I cannot skip stages of growth without being arrested in my development.

When my development as a child does not stop with my narcissistic transference, a new existential transference soon takes place. My parents, or those who take their place, become for me the temporary object of my existential striving for all goodness, truth, and beauty; I invest them with the omnipotence of Being itself. This is not surprising, for they give me all good things in life. To me they seem all-powerful and omniscient. It is true that they disappoint me at times, that I do not always receive from them what I would like, that they sometimes forbid me to do what I would like to do. At such moments of discipline and refusal, they seem to me to be all "badness." In other words, as a little child, alternating between two extremes, I experience my parents as all good or as all bad. It takes some time before I am able to integrate both aspects of the behavior of my parents into a realistic appraisal of their real worth, which is a mixture of perfection and limitation, a blend of strength and weakness, because they are not infinite goodness themselves but only limited human manifestations of God's infinite presence. As a child who cannot see this, however, my unconscious need for the Infinite inclines me to absolutize the limited qualities and defects of my parents.

Since I see them as the source and personification of all goodness, I naturally tend to identify myself with them. Man spontaneously identifies himself with pure goodness, and as soon as I feel that I have found all goodness in a person, I am unable to look for anything else. This is why heavenly creatures are so fascinated by God that they are no longer tempted by anyone or anything else. It is clear that to be fascinated in this manner by any limited person or thing on this earth would mean an encumbrance to my growth. I would be so bound to this limited appearance of goodness that I would not be sufficiently interested to search for other limited manifestations of infinite goodness. I would be unable to expand my perception of God's mysterious presence in the limited appearances of this world. Not only would I become narrow and one-sided in my captivation by this one imperfect revelation of Being, but I would not feel drawn beyond all creatures to Him to whom all creation points like one great finger.

However, the temporary identification of the child with his parents is not only unavoidable but also meaningful in this phase of his growth. It enables the child to absorb the limited values revealed in the lives of his parents. As a child I must assimilate a tremendous amount of cultural behavior, customs, knowledge, and wisdom. My parents are the representation of my culture. They are the channels through which my culture flows into me. They bear the treasures of millennia, and for me, the development of the human race is condensed in their behavior. Without them, I would be less than the cave man; with them, I am at once many thousand years old. My identification with my parents as the source of goodness, truth, and light enables me to assimilate centuries of tradition without being distracted by anything else, without questioning, and without fear. Another reason for this identification is that, without the love of my family, I would feel helpless, insecure, anxious, and forlorn in the world. If my home life is healthy and wholesome, then I find in my parents people whom I trust and love, to whom I surrender, with whom I feel secure, and who will help me if outsiders threaten me. For all these reasons, the existential transference to my parents is of unique importance.

As a matter of fact, it later becomes the prototype of existential transference to many of the significant persons in my life, such as a beloved teacher, a sweetheart, a special friend, a venerated clergyman, a superior, a mistress of novices, a confessor, or a spiritual director. My transference to them, too, is an existential transference, for I idealize them as perfect men and women. Because I see in them all goodness, truth, and light I cannot stay away from them. I like to be with them always, to obtain their special attention, to know that I have a particular place in their heart. This existential transference often reveals features of the transference which I once had to my parents. For example, I may be more inclined to develop such a transference to a man or woman who is somewhat like my father or mother. Moreover, the more insecure, uncertain, and anxious I feel, the more I am inclined to reestablish the protective and safe relationship which I once had with father and mother, who took all responsibility for my life and actions. In this case, my existential transference shows many characteristics of my childhood relationship in my family. Thus, many transferences in my later life may be called secondary existential transferences because their structure is a blend of the features of an existential transference as such and of the particular existential transference which I once had to my father and mother.

It is also quite possible that I may later develop a totally new and original existential transference to a certain person. For example, as an adolescent I may suddenly find myself in an existential transference to an inspiring teacher who opens up for me a new realm of unsuspected value and beauty. In this case, I feel a sense of adulation for the teacher, and I am rapt in ecstasy when he lectures. When I leave the classroom, I am still in the clouds, I am walking on air, for I identify my inspiring teacher with the realm of truth and beauty which he opens up to me. I am so excited and elated that I am not yet able to distinguish between him and the values of which he is the herald. It may very well be that my existential transference to him does not reveal the features of my past transference to my parents: I do not feel insecure, childlike, and in need of fatherly or motherly protection. I may not even feel inclined to speak to him personally, to be alone with him, and to seek his personal attention.

I may also develop existential transference to organizations, institutions, or countries, such as my fatherland, my city, my school, my political party, my church, or my religious order or congregation. In all these cases, I tend to idealize such organizations or institutions, to deify or divinize them. Of course, I must transcend these idealizations sooner or later, if I hope to find God Himself beyond all limitations. If I am realistic and open, my perception of reality will help me to grow beyond these immature fixations. I shall receive the wonderful gift of seeing countless imperfections and limitations in my country, in my school, in my church, in my religious order or congregation. This will be a great moment for me because, seeing in a mature way how deficient and imperfect human and religious institutions and their representatives are, I will be able to soar beyond them in search of God alone.

Each of my transferences may help me to grow by means of a temporary identification with the values embodied in the particular person or institution. Each may represent the kind of values for which I am ready at a particular phase of my maturation. All these temporary transferences are ultimately a search for Being. Because of my lack of maturity, I am unable to live these values directly in their immediacy and I must encounter them first in their embodiment in persons, symbols, and institutions.

In the series of transferences which successfully lead me to maturity, I can distinguish an idolizing and a demonizing tendency. We have seen how the limited person, symbol, institute, or occupation, which is the temporary object of my existential transference, is easily idolized as the ultimate and exclusive, as Being itself: I may deify a psychotherapist, a lecturer, a sweetheart, my own ego, or sexual pleasure as the ultimate fulfillment of my being; the object may be a "rock and roll" singer, the shining gadgets of my technical civilization, or the art of functioning smoothly within the machinery of my society. However, when I discover that these limited manifestations of Being can never fulfill my deepest longing, I may hate them in my frustration. Instead of deifying them, I may fall into the opposite excess of demonizing them. This process of a negative and demonizing transference aims at my liberation from my former positive or idolizing existential transference. At such moments, I am in a rather ambiguous and painful predicament.

For example, I have idolized my mother. But now, growing older, I discover that she is by no means the perfect person I dreamed her to be. I realize that my friends and teachers at school can give me many values that she will never be able to give me, and I feel an inner need to go beyond the ideal that her life presented to me. On the one hand I feel frustrated, disappointed, and disillusioned. I ask myself angrily how I could have been so excited about her. How could I have limited my outlook to hers? On the other hand, I still feel emotionally bound to her because I have idolized her so long and I still need her so much. Moreover, a whole world of custom, meaning, and value, *my* world is linked with my relation to her. I feel that I must grow to a wider perspective, that I must venture out in search of new horizons, but I can do so only when I free myself from my emotional fixation on my mother. Every time that I come near her, psychologically speaking, even if I try not to idolize her, I feel bound to her and lose the freedom that I need to conquer a new country of meaning. Finally, I see that my only way out is to break away from my mother emotionally. I am now inclined to exaggerate her imperfections and limitations, and I even demonize her. In doing so, however, I am able to liberate myself from her hold on my existence and to widen the horizon of my life. Sooner or later, it will no longer be necessary to see my mother in a negative light. I shall be able to see her in her real worth and value. Then I shall recognize how admirable she is within the limitations inescapable in human life. I shall recognize her virtues without falling into an unrealistic deification of her. I shall appreciate her fine qualities without being closed to those of other people, and without being blocked in my realization that God alone is perfect.

A similar situation may take place in religious life. When I am a postulant, novice, or junior, I am on a honeymoon with my religious congregation. I am inclined to identify it with all goodness, truth, and beauty. I go through a phase of idolizing transference. Later, when I become older and am immersed in the works of my congregation, I discover the manifold imperfections, human failings, and unpleasant limitations which are necessarily inherent in any human institution, even in the Church itself. At that moment I feel the pangs of dissolution, the breakdown of my idealization. I go through the pains of the negative period in religious life. Most religious people enter this stage at some time in their lives, many of them around middle age. This phase is characterized by an almost obsessive perception of flaws and frailty in the religious congregation, its policy, its superiors, and its members. At such time, I can see no good; everything seems wrong with everyone. I am fed up with this kind of religious life, and I feel that I was "taken in" during the religious honeymoon of postulancy and novitiate. Sometimes, not understanding the meaning and the purpose of this period of negative existential transference, I feel tempted to leave the congregation and to give up my vocation. I should realize, however, that this negative state is of great importance for my religious growth, that it is the prelude of a new song, the pure beginning of a melody. It is like the shedding of the cocoon, the emergence of the butterfly in the radiant light of an exciting summer.

When I know how to work through this negative period, I shall emerge into the fullness of God's light. I shall no longer do things because I want to be loved by my superior, to be praised by the people around me, or because I have the false notion that life in my community is without blemish. I shall be able at last to shed these self-deceptions and to discover God. Now, every time that I discover limitations and imperfections in my community, and in the people around me, I shall experience a deep and peaceful joy because my Beloved One alone is good and without blemish. I shall thank Him that no human being or religious community can touch His perfection, or even be compared with Him. For everyone and everything—my superiors, my fellow religious, and myself—are dust in the radiant purity of my Lord: *"Tu solus sanctus, Tu solus altissimus"*—"Thou alone art holy, Thou alone art most high." Of course, the imperfection itself of man and the world is not a cause of joy but of sadness and of attempts to improve both continuously. In the strange and beautiful logic of love, however, the lover can be enthralled by the discovery that the beloved one possesses abundantly what is lacking in himself and that he cannot transcend his own limitations without the help of his beloved. What causes his joy is not his indigence as such or the indigence of others but the increasing awareness of the infinite perfection of his creator. His growing insight into the limitations of the creatures is the occasion from which a new awareness of the radiant perfection of his Lord emerges.

To be sure, it is possible that a religious who enters this negative period may not be aware of the process of maturation that is going on in him. Something terribly unfortunate may happen to him. He may become caught in his negative existential transference. It may become a fixation. In this case, he misses the best spiritual opportunity of his life. Instead of growing to the highest presence of God beyond people, things, and institutions which he now recognizes as imperfect, he passes the second half of his life in grumbling, complaining, and carping on the faults of everyone and everything. Unhappy and disgruntled, he concentrates only on the limitations of every enterprise in which he participates.

The person who is able to live through this negative period in a wholesome way, however, will afterwards be able to rediscover the limited values which, in spite of imperfection, really exist. He will be delighted to discover so many gems of sparkling beauty in the grey mud of selfishness which spreads itself through everyday human life. The limitations which he now clearly perceives will help him to lift his heart to God, and not to make his permanent home on this earth. And the loving acts which he tenderly discovers in spite of limitations will also lift up his heart. They are for him messages of the Lord, reminders of His presence in an imperfect universe. This religious person will grow to quiet wisdom, to serene acceptance, and to a beautiful twilight in the approaching evening of his life.

The same negative process takes place in other realms of Christian life. If I am married, I shall experience the same trying period. I shall be obsessed by the shortcomings of my wife, my children, and of married life as such. If I am dedicated as a layman to a special work for the Church, as a university professor, for example, I shall eventually come face to face with an overwhelming insight into the frailty of the enterprise and the men involved in it. Similarly, I shall become aware of the limitations of my social life, my cultural interests, and my country. God may grant to anyone in any situation the grace of the dark night of negativity.

The purification of the soul of the mystic requires a further supernatural deepening of this necessary negative experience in order to free him totally from himself and from the world. The great spiritual authors have called this gift "the dark night of the soul." No growth is possible without some dark night, without an overwhelming recognition of the finiteness of others and of himself. Only such a recognition can set him free.

I shall find serenity when my existential search finally encounters God Himself and perceives in His light the relative goodness of persons and things through which He reveals and communicates His goodness to me. Then I shall be able to enjoy this relative goodness of persons and things in the light of all goodness of Being without idolizing or demonizing them. At that moment I shall have transcended the transferential state of existence.

Every existential transference leads to a change in the hierarchical mode of existence which is my existential project. The mode of existence toward the idolized person or object becomes central and tends to influence the other modes of existence which become more peripheral. Moreover, a certain existential transference may be strong and dominant in a particular culture. For example, in our culture the existential transference to status symbols, such as college degrees from ivy league institutions, the latest model car with excessively large fenders, success in the market of weekly dates for young people, may easily take the place of true inner values and arrest the growth toward maturity in those who become addicted to empty symbols of inauthentic prestige.

If I am caught in such an existential fixation common to my culture, then transcending my existential transference also implies transcending my culture. This is a problem not only for the growth of the authentic Christian in the world but also for the Christian who chooses the religious way of life, for he enters this life bearing the wounds of the fixation of his culture. He may unwittingly live an unauthentic project of life within his religious community. For him the atmosphere has changed, but the drive for status symbols remains the same. If he searches his soul, he may be surprised by the unmistakable symptoms of the cultural disease. He may discover in himself the hidden desire to become a superior, or he may be jealous of his colleagues who gain glory as speakers, teachers, or writers because he himself hungers for status and prestige. He may also find that much of his behavior is motivated, at least in part, by the desire to appear superior to others. If such a person is unable to obtain recognition by means of special talents, or if he is too lax to engage in the exhausting work that would earn him recognition, he may be devoured by the secret wish to become a director or an important administrator of an institution. As long as this religious person has not plumbed the depth of his cultural disease, his spiritual life will be a farce. He will be unable to develop a real, mature presence to God because his cultural fixation on status symbols will make it impossible for him to prefer God to his ambition.

Of course, there is no fault in the person who knows objectively that he can best serve others by humbly fulfilling the exacting demands of administration. Good, self-forgetting, hard-working administrators fulfill a necessary task in the Church and in society. They create the climate and the conditions within which others can fulfill their tasks and achieve the objectives of the community. Creative and broad-minded administrators are needed—people who regard their office not as a symbol of status but as a manner of serving God and the world most effectively. Such administrators are not caught in existential fixation on prestige symbols.

THE PROPER PHASE OF RELIGIOUS DEVELOPMENT

Thus far we have concentrated chiefly on the preparatory phase of religious development. We have called it preparatory because so long as I am in the process of search for the proper object of my religious mode of existence, I do not yet enjoy religious growth in the deepest sense of the word. However, the preparatory stage in my religious life can really lead to the moment in which I find God in people, things, and events. As soon as I see God in all things, as soon as I no longer experience them as ultimate in my life, I am ready for religious growth in the most proper sense. To be sure, there is no clear-cut separation between the preparatory stages of my religious growth and its proper development because a religious person also lives for God in the preparatory phase which disposes him for his full religious development. Even when I am involved in existential transference to my mother, my teacher, or my religious community, I do not stop loving God, going to Church, saying my prayers. Indeed, I may be truly religious during my existential transferences. The difference between this time and the later full development of my religious life is mainly that the religious mode of existence is not yet able to permeate completely my other modes of existence. As a result, I do not yet achieve a perfect unity and simplicity of personality. My religious mode of life and my passing fascination with people and institutions which fill me with so much admiration exist, as it were, side by side. They do not permeate each other; in fact, most of the time they are isolated from each other. Nevertheless, my fascination with people or events makes it impossible for me to be wholeheartedly, simply, and exclusively directed toward God. At times my enthusiasm for the earth may be so strong that I forget about heaven.

Neither is the full presence of my life to God a sudden event without previous history. Already during the preparatory phase the introduction to a full presence to the divine takes place. Especially toward the end of this stage, there are moments of sudden light in which the veil drops from my eyes, in which I experience at once the limitation of all earthly things and the hunger for the Infinite. If I am faithful to this movement of grace, such sporadic moments will repeat themselves, their duration will be lengthened, and my desire will deepen. In the meantime, the series of positive and negative existential transferences continues. Each new period of negativity, when lived through with the proper attitude, liberates me somewhat more from myself and my myopic view of creatures. Finally, this increasing liberation, combined with the increasing growth of moments of light, will lead to a full presence to the divine. Then I am ready at last to experience my religious mode of existence, not only as the most central one in my project of existence, but also as the actual permeation of all my other modes of being in the world. No one or nothing can any longer fascinate me to such a degree that I forget that God is my first love in all things. Now I may deeply enjoy teaching, traveling, art, nature, professional success, or certain people without losing my loving presence to my Lord. Now I find Him everywhere, in a human face, the song of a bird, a delightful novel, an impressive opera, or a charming companion.

When I have reached this grace of full presence, is my religious development now finished? Does my full presence to God always have the same character? Or can this presence also grow in depth? In other words, does my presence to God have its own stages of development?

If I ask myself this question, I am no longer asking to whom my mode of existence is directed or oriented. Neither am I asking how I as an individual live this mode of existence or how it is lived in my culture. It is certainly true that every mode of existence—including the full presence to God—has a unique character in each individual and also a cultural character. But the question I now ask is, what are the possible levels of development through which my presence to God may grow to fullness and perfection? To state it in another way, the psychological structure of a mode of existence consists of various constitutents: (1) teleological, or the directedness of the mode of existence toward its object; (2) individual, or the unique way in which one stands out toward this object; (3) cultural, or the intersubjectively shared mode of standing out toward the object; and, (4) the developmental constituent. The latter is dependent upon the over-all level of existence which I have reached in my individual development. Quite obviously it affects my mode of full presence to God. It is clear, for instance, that a saintly child who is fully present to God is present to Him in a different manner than a saintly old man. The same may be said of an adolescent girl as compared to an adult woman. During the actualization of my life, I successively reach different levels of existence, and every level which I achieve leads to a different style of religious life, a new way of being present to the divine.

We may distinguish four levels of existence: the biosensual, the functional, the romantic, and the existential. The last is called existential, not because the others are not levels of human existence, but because on this level the typical human or existential character is most clearly and predominantly present. Therefore, this highest level of being is "existential" par excellence.

My biosensual level of existence is dominated by biosensual needs and makes for the discovery of a world of people and things that alleviate bodily needs and desires. The religious mode of existence of persons living on this level has strong sensual characteristics, which can be observed in the religiosity of children and certain primitive tribes. This level of existence does not exclude the higher levels, which are always implicitly and vaguely present, though far from predominant, in the subject. When a person excludes these higher levels, however, his religious mode of existence may deteriorate. The repression of the higher levels may even lead, under religious pretexts, to psychopathological perversion in sex, food, drink, and drugs.

The functional level of existence is the ego level, the level of mastery, control, organization, technique, of having and possessing. The religious mode of existence lived at this level reveals such characteristics as pragmatic concern with numerous religious practices; hair-splitting attention to the details of the moral code; constant prayer for practical favors like good weather, success in examinations, a new car, or a well-paying job. When this level excludes openness for higher levels, it may lead to moral fanaticism, witch-hunting, a holier-than-thou attitude, and the perversion of the religious mode of existence into religious materialism and scientism.

The romantic level of existence develops under the influence of overwhelming emotional experience which at once impels man out of his self-centered biosensual, functional existence, making him deeply aware of the not-self. Without this experience, certain persons may never escape their narrow prison of self-centeredness in which they are condemned to an impoverished existence. The romantic experience temporarily produces an attitude of delight in beholding the goodness and perfection of God. The romantic religious mode of existence manifests itself in religious fascination, exaltation, rapture, and extremely affectionate prayer. Bodily manifestations of emotion, such as changes in pulse rate and heartbeat, are clearly present. When this romantic level excludes other levels, the romantic religious phase becomes a curse instead of a blessing. And when this delightful religious fascination becomes a fixation, an isolated aim, it unavoidably deteriorates, and man's whole religious life shares in its degeneration. Religion becomes a self-deceptive cultivation of religious moods and feelings. This degenerated, inauthentic form of religious existence, instead of lifting man beyond himself, instead of widening and deepening his being and breaking down his fruitless isolation, confines him more than ever within a self-centered universe of artificially maintained affections. Instead of finding communion with Being in existential participation, he finds only his own unhappy self, starved for a participation which constantly eludes him. For him, religious existence has lost its meaning; it has become a fantasy, an illusion. His attitude may become psychopathological if it leads him to a hysterical search for manifestations of religious emotion.

The romantic religious mode of existence has its roots in man's being, which is dynamic and self-actualizing. All man's authentic experience relates in some way to his self-realization, but there is a hierarchy among the crucial phenomena of this development. According to this hierarchy, the lower phenomena of self-actualization receive their deepest significance from the higher phenomena. The lower, in fact, serve to prepare man's being for the higher. Religious romanticism is not a permanent state but a passing experience, beautiful but brief, like the quick glimpse of a bird in flight past our open window on a lovely spring morning. Its very fleetness implies that the romantic religious experience cannot be a lasting and definite fulfillment of man's being. But neither is the romantic religious experience a meaningless incident in the development of the religious mode of existence, a momentary excitement that leaves no trace in man's religious life. Lacking a lasting and final meaning in itself, it receives its meaning from a higher form of self-actualization and religious participation, a higher form of living. The deepest meaning of the authentic religious romantic experience is to dispose the person for a deeper mode of religious existence, which is a truly existential commitment. Religious enchantment serves as a prelude, an overture, and manifests itself as an overwhelming appeal to escape self-centeredness in order to center one's existence in Being as it reveals itself. Once the appeal has been issued, once the prelude of religious existence has illuminated the being of man and redeemed him momentarily from himself, the stage is set for religious commitment.

The early phases of transition from feeling to full commitment may prove sad and melancholic, for the beauty of religious enchantment fades before the fullness of existential religious commitment is experienced. The romantic religious mode of existence is somewhat peripheral. It is experienced as a free gift, a complete surprise, a sudden burst of joy and light. It therefore manifests itself most strongly in the emotional aesthetic sphere. Because this sphere lies near the core of man's existence, the experience can be a suggestion, an appeal to the very center of man's being. Yet it remains only an appeal and does not penetrate his most inner self, the region of fundamental commitment. The existential religious mode of being, on the other hand, is the very depth of man's existence responding to this appeal. In the center of his existence man must answer, must commit himself, must decide whether or not he will ex-ist, stand out with his whole being toward the infinite transcendent Being experienced by him as his last Ground. It is a psychological law that the experience of appeal follows unavoidably the romantic religious experience.

Passivity predominates in the psychology of romantic religious existence, for this is an appeal rather than an answer, an overpowering experience rather than an active commitment, fascination rather than creative care. Psychological analysis of existential religious commitment, on the other hand, reveals it to be realistic, core penetrating, and actively creative. It tends to embody itself concretely in the whole of man's daily life.

This religious mode of being may be described psychologically as an *existential* commitment for four reasons. It is ex-istential in so far as it is a commitment to ex-ist, literally to stand out beyond one's self toward a personal Transcendent who is experienced as the Ground of one's being. This is an existential commitment par excellence because it forces the subject to forego many other ways of relating to people and things, which might prove incompatible with the new dominant way of standing out toward the experienced Transcendent. This commitment is primarily existential, moreover, because it takes place within the central core of one's being and because it implies a readiness to dedicate one's whole life, all actions, thoughts, and feelings, to the Transcendent. The *actual* dedication of existence, of course, depends on the concrete situation, but the *readiness* for dedication permeates the life core of the religious person.

Having explained the meaning of *existential* in the psychological expression, "mode of religious existential commitment," we may now clarify the main term, *commitment*. The religious mode of being as existential commitment is something quite different from feeling, affection, or emotion. It is a mode of being in which one accepts without reservation the experienced Transcendent and the reality which He permits to be. Psychologically, then, it is an accepted and lovingly cultivated union with Transcendent Being, an unconditional standing out toward Him and toward that which is experienced as His will. This commitment implies, therefore, the abandonment of one's autonomous, self-sufficient existence in order to participate willingly in Being as it reveals itself in one's concrete life situation. Briefly, the religious mode as commitment is experienced as the free gift of one's whole being to the Transcendent, whom one encounters as the unique one who can fulfill one's being. This commitment uncovers for the subject a world in which the Transcendent is ever more and more present.

THE PHASE OF INCARNATION OF RELIGIOUS DEVELOPMENT

We have described the transferential and developmental growth of the religious mode of existence and may now consider the psychology of the final, never-ending phase of growth in the religious mode of life, which we shall call the phase of *incarnation* or embodiment.

We have seen that the religious mode of being is called existential in so far as it is a commitment deep within the subject, there where man is most authentically himself, where he experiences himself as free. We have also noted that "existential" implies, psychologically, a commitment of the whole existence of the subject, of his life and body, of his thoughts and emotions, interests and activities. However, the actualization of this commitment is experienced as never finished, never perfect, as frequently discontinued and sometimes threatened. Though the religious commitment is rooted primarily in the free center of man's existence, many feelings, thoughts, imaginations, desires, and habits are not always experienced as free. Man cannot force them at will in all situations. His psychological world is the totality of "evaluated" people and things which play potential or actual roles in his existence. Their significance determines psychologically his ways of behaving. His behavior, therefore, may be called psychologically free, first, in so far as he himself experiences himself as free in his evaluation of people and things, and second, in so far as his patterns of behavior gradually respond to these evaluations. By changing himself he changes his behavior. When man functions normally, therefore, a dependent relationship exists between his behavior and his world of meaning.

Now, the man who commits himself religiously in the depth of his being changes psychologically the meaning of his world; it becomes a religious world. But this change requires time, for it implies that other worlds of meaning will be relegated to a more peripheral place in his existential project, and even that some worlds of meaning which are incompatible with his religious world will be discarded. This is a time-consuming process. By choosing a new world

of meaning which he discovers in reality as a result of a new mode
of existence, man exposes his behavior to conditioning by new,
freely chosen signs. Once a man has uncovered this new religious
world and has changed his behavior in response to it, many of his
everyday responses are to a remarkable degree automatic, conditioned by the signs he himself has erected. The psychological
observation of behavior reveals that a new religious evaluation of
people and things is followed by a change in the conditional responses of the subject. But, again, this change is not possible all at
once. After his basic option of a new existential project, man must
overcome his former ties to conditioned responses that were predominant when other modes of existence were central in his existential project.

Therefore, the primordial option "to-be-for-the-Transcendent,"
taken once and for all in the core of man's being, can only gradually expand its influence to the peripheral regions of attitudes, feelings, desires, thoughts, habits, and actions which are still conditioned
by signs of other worlds of human meaning and purpose.

The religious mode of existence, then, does not mean psychologically that the person is from now on always attracted by the Transcendent, that he always "feels" his religious commitment, that he
is never tempted to betray it, that he never *feels* angry with God,
or that he never fails. According to psychological observation,
existential religious commitment grants no such guarantee. Temptation, anger, resistance, weakness, and failure may emerge in the
more peripheral regions of man's existence, but they cannot directly
destroy the existential religious commitment which maintains itself
in the core of his being. On the other hand, an authentic religious
mode of existence implies a continual willingness to pervade these
remote areas of existence more and more with the light and inspiration of this primordial commitment. Such a manner of life may be
defined psychologically as an everlasting, unconditional readiness to
restore the religious attitude in all the regions of a person's being
whenever this attitude is impaired by weakness, laxity, and failure,
or threatened by temptation and doubt. Consequently, religious
commitment implies a life-long growth in the actualization of this
commitment in thoughts, feelings, desires, and actions. At the same
time, the primordial religious commitment in the center of existence

is reinforced every time the person has to reassert it, to reconfirm it after the experience of temptation, indifference, disappointment, or failure. Temptations and failures, in fact, strengthen the religious commitment, which reinforces itself by repeated self-assertion. Such habitual self-assertion in adverse situations finally makes for that unshakably solid quality of religious existence that may be observed in the behavior of certain older people who have constantly reinforced their religious mode of existence during a lifetime of trials and temptations.

Thus, existential religious commitment does not imply—as aesthetic, emotional religion does—that the person always consciously feels his commitment. Conscious feeling belongs to the more peripheral regions of life. The "feel" of religious commitment, therefore, may be lacking, especially after failure or temptation, or during concentrated attention to other matters. Yet the commitment expresses itself psychologically in a behavior that always seeks the restoration of the religious mode of existence and does not rest until the influence of this central mode is restored as far as possible in the peripheral modes which help to constitute the person's full project of being.

This fundamental readiness, which flows immediately from the commitment of one's whole being to the Personal Transcendent, reveals and embodies itself in four basic attitudes toward the Transcendent and His presence. These are acceptance, self-actualizing surrender, fidelity, and creative care.

The attitude of *acceptance* is a lasting readiness to accept the Transcendent and that which is experienced as His will in one's concrete life situation without denying, repressing, or resisting this reality. Certain distressing life situations may tempt the religious person to reject this attitude. But unconditional commitment enables him to accept reality, even when he is affected painfully in the less central regions of his being. He is possessed of a lasting faith in the mysterious benevolence of the Transcendent, even when painful crises cloud his experience of God's presence in the everyday world.

The attitude of *self-actualizing surrender* arises from the authentic gift of oneself, which implies growth in maturity by constant participation in the Transcendent and His dynamically developing world. The continual readiness to investigate the source of every failure to accept the concrete reality in which the Transcendent reveals Himself makes the religious person more and more aware of his hidden defenses, his unconscious anxieties, his withholding of himself, and his lurking hostility, distrust, and bitterness in certain regions of his being. These weaknesses do not make the religious commitment psychologically impossible, but they impair the actualization of the religious mode of existence in thoughts, feelings, and acts. The religious mode implies the readiness to change gradually in oneself any obstacle to the full dominance of this mode over all other modes in one's existential project. When this readiness is not successfully achieved, there may still be commitment; but when this readiness itself is totally and continuously absent, the religious mode of existence is psychologically no longer possible.

The attitude of *fidelity* belongs to the fundamental psychological structure of religious commitment, for without this all-pervading attitude of unconditional loyalty the religious mode of life is psychologically impossible. Whether the person experiences health or sickness, poverty or wealth, success or failure, excitement or dreariness, understanding or misunderstanding, he always maintains deep within him this unyielding engagement to be faithful to the commitment once promised. It is a hallmark of the psychology of the religiously committed person, no matter to what faith he adheres. Fidelity in everyday life means that the religious person will reinforce his attitude toward the Transcendent as soon as he discovers that his religious mode of existence is becoming weak, stale, or routine, or is threatened by temptation. Fidelity is, psychologically speaking, a readiness for every sacrifice necessary to preserve the original commitment. Psychological analysis reveals to us that this fidelity also implies vigilance against such intense absorption in other interests that the person cannot maintain his presence to the Transcendent as He reveals Himself in daily experience. No way of ex-isting, of standing out in the person's existential project, will become so predominant that it prevents standing out primarily toward the Transcendent and His presence in reality. To make the peripheral modes within his existential project central would be experienced by the religious person as a betrayal of the fidelity which flows from his central commitment to relate to the Transcendent as first in his life.

The attitude of *creative care* is the readiness to care for the reality in which the Transcendent is revealed within the world of the religious person. This continual concern for one's own reality and the reality which appears in one's situation includes a solicitude not only for spiritual life but for all conditions which may foster the authentic growth of oneself and others, such as concern for culture, science, social improvement, physical fitness, and even relaxation and entertainment. The commitment to the Transcendent thus becomes a commitment to both the spiritual and the material good of all in the never finished phase of incarnation of the religious mode of existence.

DEVIATIONS
of the Religious Personality

4

AFTER CONSIDERING the psychological structure and development of the religious mode of existence, it is a relatively simple task to indicate the main areas within this development where psychopathological attitudes and symptoms may develop.

Existential psychopathology may be defined as a fundamental disharmony of existence, which is due to a persistent lack of integration of different modes of existence and which manifests itself in some kind of psychopathological behavior. Existential psychopathology of the religious mode of life may consequently be defined as a fundamental disharmony of existence due to a persistent lack of integration of the religious mode with other modes of existence and leading to psychopathological symptoms. Our definition stresses that the disharmony must be fundamental and not temporary or incidental, even when protracted over a certain period of time. The lack of harmony is called fundamental only when it is, as it were, a fixated disharmony that permanently permeates the whole psychological make-up of the person, who in no way grows to a solution of this discordance. We call it a disharmony of *existence* because it is a conflict between modes of life which, in their temporary state, are incompatible with one another but which are nevertheless maintained together by the same person. In other words, the person has developed a schizoid existential project, so that he attempts to stand out in reality in ways which are incompatible with one another. We speak of existential psychopathology only when this persistent lack of integration leads to psychopathological symptoms.

We do not deny, of course, that the lack of integration is already present before it manifests itself in symptoms, but the psychologist can verify this lack of integration only if it manifests itself in some way in observable behavior. It is evident that there are other causes of psychopathological behavior than a fundamental disharmony of existence. Therefore, we restrict ourselves here to what we call existential psychopathology. Frequently, other causes of psychopathology may interact with existential causes or even lead to fundamental disharmony. A brain-damaged patient, for example, who is not willing to accept his restricted possibilities of existence may develop a fundamental disharmony within his existential project and thereby aggravate his symptoms.

In what ways can a persistent and fundamental conflict between the religious and other modes of existence develop? There are two possibilities: the religious mode does not integrate the other modes of life but represses them; or, the other modes of existence repress the religious mode. Repression means, not that the modes of life themselves are gradually discarded, but that only the clear awareness of these modes is rejected while they themselves are still dynamic and active but beyond the control of the subject.

FIXATIONS IN THE BIOSENSUAL, FUNCTIONAL, ROMANTIC, AND INCARNATIVE PHASES OF RELIGIOUS DEVELOPMENT

The religious mode of existence may be fundamentally incapable of integrating the other modes because it is not open toward its own object but fixated on some object that is idolized. This attitude leads to the repression of those spontaneous and natural ways of life which would expose the unrealistic mode of existence.

This type of fundamental disharmony may establish itself in the preparatory transferential stage of religious development. When the existential idolizing transference is not a passing event but becomes a fixation, then it blocks all growth in personal insight, selfhood, and independency which would normally lead to the experience that parents or parental figures, for example, are not godlike, perfect beings. If this spontaneous insight develops nevertheless on the prereflective level of existence, it will be repressed by the idolizing fixation and will cause constant tension, guilt, and anxiety in the person.

On the other hand, when the fixation takes place during the negative demonizing transference, then the subject identifies the object of the religious mode of existence with the demonized narcissistic self, or the demonized parents, parental figures, clergymen, or religious institutes. If, however, the religious quest remains present, it will be repressed by the demonizing fixation and cause tension, guilt, and anxiety. The same may be said of the proper stage of development of the religious mode of existence.

A fixation on the biosensual stage of existence may give rise to a frantic psychopathological pursuit of sensual experiences in order to fulfill the need for religious participation. It is important here to distinguish among an immature, a vulgar, and a neurotic existence.

An immature existence stands out in reality on a relatively lower level, not because of repression, but because of failure to reach full maturity. The individual simply lacks the inner and outer historical and environmental conditions necessary for the development of higher modes of existence. Certain primitive cultures, for example, manifest a religious life that is very much colored by the pursuit of biosensual experiences, such as uninhibited sexual intercourse, drunkenness, and hysterical bodily gyrations, as part of the religious rites of the tribe.

A vulgar existence, on the other hand, is one in which a higher level of being has announced itself but has been repressed in such an absolute and efficient manner that the person is not disturbed by any symptoms which betray the repression. Such a life is vulgar in so far as the repression reveals itself in a continual, sometimes aggressive defensiveness against any reminder of a higher possibility of living. For example, a person may possess a deep sensitivity to poetry and music, but repress it so thoroughly that he is not aware of it and is even outspokenly averse to all poetic or musical expression.

A neurotic existence, finally, is one which has failed to repress completely the higher modes of existence which continue to build prereflectively a world which the person fears. The tension between the world in which the person tries to live and the repressed world which keeps building itself leads to psychopathological symptoms. Therefore, when we speak here about psychopathology of religion, we always presuppose that the existential fixation on an object of transference or a level of existence is preceded and accompanied by an existential repression of another object or another level which has already announced itself prereflectively. We presuppose, moveover, that this repression is no longer completely successful.

A fixation on the functional level of existence leads to a functionalized religious life of a compulsive nature or to the repression of the religious quest. As we have already seen, the cultural mode of existence or cultural fixations deeply influence the personal mode of existence. The contemporary Western mode of standing out is predominantly functional and easily leads, therefore, to an embarrassed repression of religious awareness. The predominance of the functional fixation in our Western culture impels us to expand our discussion of this contemporary situation.

With the dawn of the Industrial Revolution, profit-making became one of the main purposes of existence in the Western world, and spontaneous human cooperation was consequently submerged in a scheme of functional interaction. As a result, entire generations concentrated their energy, not on the cultivation of the inner self, but on the development of the marketable skills which are predominant at the functional level of existence. Within modern organizations, the human person disappeared like a little card in the dull anonymity of a monstrous file. Cities and metropolises proliferated wherever large numbers of faceless people banded together as strangers with no common convictions, roots, or traditions. The standardized school emerged in which children of families with basically different roots and convictions drilled together in specific marketable skills. This standardized school of the capitalistic community was unable to integrate its training within the traditions of the generations which preceded it, for the traditions which were highly respected in one family were thoroughly despised by its neighbors. The result was a historically unique and frightening anomaly: The education of new generations became for the first time in history a standardized drill in skills, techniques, and factual information with no link whatever to the dynamic springs of tradition. Technical generations were trained which had lost their contact with the past and drifted without values on the treacherous currents of fashionable feelings and chance impressions. Thus, the technical barbarian was born. The standardized school had become a phantom ship with a crew more skillfull, clever, and technical than ever before, but without helm, compass, or harbor. Instead of a harmoniously developed community, a homogeneous mass emerged. To be like the successful man next door, to attain the same material objectives as the other, became for many the shallow measure of living.

Contemporary man's mode of existence is predominantly functional, and this technical appreciation of nature and reality is early imposed on the awareness of the younger members of the culture. Under the impact of this early education of his awareness, man is inclined to perceive the world as his civilization thinks it to be. The result is an estrangement from true nature in its natural totality, and man comes to experience nature as a thing, a storehouse of measurable power, a field of exploitation. A river, for example, is perceived predominantly as a means of transportation or as a source of energy—a phenomenon whose meaning must be some kind of utility. Consequently, functional man is unable to absorb the radiant message of beauty, grandeur, and mystery which reveals itself only to that openness in wonder which is no longer awakened because of a utilitarian education.

In a predominantly functional society, the full experience of the world as it manifests itself is often degraded to mere information. This functional mode of existence does not allow the growth of man's personal self, which remains submerged under the unassimilated burden of factual information. An inauthentic self, a common kind of pragmatic ego feeding with millions of others on the same superficial information, becomes the hidden source of dull conformity in reactions and evaluations among a faceless crowd. The awareness of the functional man is overalert at its periphery, but vague and disintegrated at its center. The neat, compulsive organization of the world within categories at the periphery of man's awareness is offset by anarchy at the core of his being, which is a whirlpool of unclarified wishes, vague fantasies, and conflicting ideas. Emotional repression is the central force in the make-up of functional man, without which it would be impossible for him to narrow down the vision of the world to its mere technical dimensions. Finally, the periphery of awareness becomes the dominant force in his life, while the core of consciousness becomes unconscious and can manifest itself only in disturbing dreams and neurotic symptoms.

When the fullness of awareness is diminished to an exclusive awareness of unrelated masses of useful information, then the inwardness of man is soon filled with unassimilated scraps and morsels of a world that eludes him in its mystery. The self of the functional man cannot open up in wonder to the mystery of Being, and his inner life shrivels to a mere reflex of the artificial prison shaped by selective perception. No surprise, no beauty, no mystery is left for the functional awareness which is compulsively absorbed in the measurable aspects of the world.

The attitude of a contemporary man can be described as a vague, inactive resignation. As a functional existence without deep self-awareness, he is unable to take a position toward a self that is absent. Being a reflection of his artificial universe, the functional man is almost totally incapable of self-reflection. Being a stranger to himself, no norms are revealed to him in the innermost reaches of his being. Such a man, hyperorganized in his scientific and professional life, is confused and disharmonious in his private sphere of living. Often a mere functionary, who has shriveled to an empty ego, he is unable to encounter the divine. Religious transcendence is unknown to a pragmatic ego entangled in a web of functional ties involving it continuously in short-range projects and sordid trivialities. And so, as the religious need does not announce itself to prereflective awareness, no conflict is experienced between the predominant social and the personal modes of existence.

When, however, the religious interest arises in certain individuals with a functional background, they feel unconsciously embarrassed, ashamed, anxious, and guilty about this deviation from the cultural code. This guilt leads to a strongly organized defensive behavior. The defense may become an all-pervasive nihilism, an anxiously debunking, nothing-but attitude, a reduction of all possible values to nothingness. A person who thus protects himself against the religious mode of existence may depreciate himself as nothing but a stimulus-response mechanism without responsibility; he may view the universe as a rather boring cluster of atoms and molecules without meaning or purpose; love, as an agreeable disturbance of his chemistry; arts and sciences, as fancy sublimations of the sex drive; human history, as nothing but a dull process with the regularity of a clock, based on the iron laws of economic determinism. This defensive nihilism poisons his existential project; it dries up in him all life and enthusiasm, reverence, wonder, and commitment. It may easily lead to anxiety, depression, despair, and defeatism. The unconscious aim of such defensive nihilism is to make certain that threatening religious values are reduced, like everything else, to nothingness.

The repression is not always successful. The person can muffle but not always nullify the silent voice of his prereflective existence. His attempt to escape this call cannot silence its steady invitation, but can only distort its message. His consequent misunderstanding of the muzzled whisper of existence leads to the perversion of the religious quest. In this case, the person may develop a habit of compulsive functioning, a neurotic involvement in never-ending activities, as if he could fill the inner void by the quantity of work done. On the other hand, when he becomes older he may experience his fruitless functioning as a useless passion. He may be reminded of a match lighted for a fleeting moment by a playing child and thrown on the pavement to die out meaninglessly the next second. In extreme cases such a person, overcome by the uselessness of his life, may commit suicide.

Another type of functional man may belong to a church, but the subtle sensitivity that kept his believing forebears in tune with religious values has degenerated in him from lack of use in his functional universe. He may still manifest piety in the shadow of the pulpit, but his piety is somewhat schizoid. There is a split between his pragmatic ego on the functional level and his undeveloped self on the existential level. The latter he tries to excite during a Sunday morning hour, putting it cautiously back on the shelf for the rest of the week. There is no living unity between his incidental attempts to be religious somewhere at the fringe of his existential project and his daily existence where the functional mode is central. The predominant functional attitude easily overpowers the weak religious stirrings. Then, his church activity shrinks into another formality within the scheme of social things one does—nobody knows why—in his society. The impossibility, however, of coming to an integrated project of existence because of this split between the functional and the religious may lead to psychopathological symptoms, such as morbid anxiety, guilt, and tension.

The rebellion against functionalism under the impact of the distorted religious quest may lead to other psychopathological attitudes and symptoms. The nihilism of functional man is a reduction of all religious values to pragmatic relationships. The nihilism of the person who rebels against functionalism, however, and who still does not discover his repressed religious awareness, becomes a resentful denial of all forms of culture, and especially of the technical civilization which betrayed his original trust. Overwhelmed by cultural pessimism, he may regress to the biosensual level of being. He feels obsessed by a sickening doubt about all meaning and all culture and about their sources: reason and intuition. He becomes an easy prey of irrational romanticism, vitalism, or back-to-nature mysticism. He may ridicule and reject all the cultural embodiments of creative intuition, functional reason, and tradition in society. He may even become fanatic about the big bomb which promises to blow to pieces a civilization which he experiences as meaningless. It becomes impossible for him to conceive that functional thinking and technique can be wisely integrated with spontaneity, inspiration, and creativity in a mature existence. Rebellious romanticism or sensualism blinds him to the possibility of wholesome integrations of prayer and practice, humanism and technique, logic and inspiration, life and civilization. In other words, the disillusioned functional man does not hope or strive for the emergence of the human self which will pervade, enrich, and inspire his functional intelligence and his biosensual sphere. On the contrary, he posits an unbridgeable gap between bios and logos.

The predominance of the functional attitude in contemporary culture may lead to a fixation even in the person who is wholly dedicated to the development of a religious mode of being. In this case, the perversion of the religious quest may lead to psychopathological symptoms. The religious subject who attempts to fulfill his quest for Infinite Being by means of only functional activities deteriorates into a fanatic observer of a rigid code of numerous do's and don'ts in the unconscious hope of thus mastering the Transcendent and His benevolence. A failure to fulfill any of these tiny prescripts results in tension, unbearable guilt feelings, and neurotic self-rejection. Life may become sheer torture for such a person.

We have seen that the religious romantic experience is an invitation to existential religious commitment. In the normal case, romantic religious existence, having fulfilled its mission in the development of the individual, recedes, while existential commitment predominates. Romantic religious existence, however, becomes inauthentic when its natural disappearance is not accepted, when it is artificially forced to continue and becomes an aim in itself. Then it deteriorates unavoidably, and man's whole being shares in its degeneration. Religious life becomes a cultivation of pious moods and feelings, and the world becomes a universe of artificially maintained, devout sentimentality which casts its spell over people, things, and events.

A degenerated romantic religious existence loses its inner orientation toward Transcendent Being, whose implicit revelation was paradoxically the hidden source of the original sublimity of this religious affection. The repeated attempt to recapture the original religious rapture cannot force its source, the spontaneous awareness of the Transcendent. As a result, inauthentic experiential substitutes are sought, and the affective dimension of the religious experience now becomes its exclusive content. The hungry striving of the person for religious emotion degenerates into a search for pious sentimentality, kept alive by saccharine symbolism embodied in cheap sentimental prayer, sculpture, painting, poetry, and song. At the same time, the unconscious identification of religious existence with emotional elation arouses feelings of guilt, anxiety, and despair when these feelings are absent. The craving for religious emotionality and its exhibition in behavior may even cause hysterical symptoms in this person, just as fixation on the functional level may lead to a predominantly compulsive symptomatology.

Another form of fixation is that of religious aestheticism. The lovelier and more alluring an object of fixation, the stronger its hold on its victim. Psychotherapeutic experience reveals how difficult it is to widen the obsessive perception of a person who lives under the spell of religious aestheticism. For such a person, religion has become an aesthetic event. He absolutizes the aesthetic experience and its symbolic expression. This fixation not only blocks his growth toward a deeper religious commitment but also closes him to the relative values of the lower modes of existence, such as the functional and pragmatic, without which man cannot live soundly and wholly. He may deny and despise everything that is not aesthetic and thus involve himself in numerous clashes with his fellow men. Religious aestheticism, when absolutized, may ruin the person's realistic perception of man and the world. It may make him nervous and tense, bitter and resentful. Finally, it may distort or even destroy the aesthetic religious experience itself by the constant neglect of the pragmatic, biological, and social conditions necessary for wholesome experience. The man who makes the aesthetic experience his god by making it ultimate may suffer the same neurotic distortions as the man who transfers his search for Being to his mother or to his therapist. The aesthetic fixation, however, is not at all inevitable. If the religious aesthetic experience matures normally, then there will emerge during the joyful, reverent communion with art and nature a deep awareness of an infinite Presence behind order, beauty, and harmony, an immediate experience of the Holy filled with an intimate certitude which may lead to existential commitment.

As we have seen, existential commitment in the center of a person's being strives to embody itself gradually in the more peripheral areas of his life. This embodiment realizes itself not by repression but by the gradual development and integration of modes of existence which are compatible with the religious mode, and by the lack of reinforcement of modes of existence which are incompatible with this central attitude. In the meantime, concrete motivation and behavior remain the expression of all the modes of existence which are still active in the person. Therefore, the actual motivation and behavior of the average religious person are usually not *purely* religious. The healthy person accepts this fact humbly and develops a realistic existential project which is in tune with his concrete life situation. He perceives realistically the necessary gradualness of the actualization of his existence, and he accepts religiously the fact that the Transcendent made man in such a way that a sudden actualization of his existence is impossible. He is not appalled, therefore, when he discovers some lingering influence of incompatible modes of existence in his own religious motivation and behavior.

The person who develops in a less wholesome way, however, does not adapt his concrete existential project to his real situation. His project loses its moorings in reality and becomes an ideal of perfection impossible to fulfill. Sometimes the cultural mode of existence in his environment is the cause of this exalted religious idealism. And the response of the person to his subsequent failure to fulfill this obsessive religious project of existence can well be unbearable guilt and depression accompanied by self-rejection. In others, the continual pressure may lead to a total rejection of all religion in order to escape the burden of an impossible perfection. This rejection is usually a form of repression, which means that the repressed demand for religious perfection may express itself in severe psychopathological symptoms. Others, again, in order to escape the same pressure, identify their own reality with their unrealistic existential project. That is, they develop an "as if" existence. They talk, smile, act, and display piety as if they had fully realized their impossible project. Everything that would expose this illusion is rationalized in such a way that it harmonizes with their conviction. For example, when other people show irritation with their behavior, it is explained as the kind of persecution which has been suffered by saintly persons. The repressed modes of existence reveal themselves in distorted ways: aggression and hostility, for example, appear as an aggressive kind of apostolate and a moralizing tendency. Envy and jealousy manifest themselves as pious concern for the purity of motivation in religious persons who are more successful than the inauthentic person himself. Repressed social ambitions reveal themselves in a compulsive need to be an outstanding observer of religious rules. It sometimes happens that such a person develops paranoid symptoms. If unexpected traumatic experiences make him suddenly aware of the falsehood of religious life, a severe break-down may be inevitable.

Another possible source of psychopathology during the phase of existential embodiment may be found in the denial of modes of being which are compatible with a religious project of life and which should therefore be integrated within a wholesome project of exist-ence. Here, too, the cultural project may be influential. When a culture, for example, is negative in its attitude toward the arts and sciences, religious groups of people may translate this rejection into a conviction that the arts and sciences are incompatible with holi-ness. This denial may eventually cause tension and conflict, especially in those members of the religious groups who feel a natural affinity to the arts and sciences, and who cannot long tolerate this sick repression. Many cultural influences of the past few centuries, es-pecially the Cartesian dualism predominant in the West, have con-tributed to the severe psychopathology observed so frequently in religious groups of people who have been unable to embody their religion in a natural and healthy way in their personalities.

NEUROTIC TENDENCIES IN THE STRIVING
FOR RELIGIOUS PERFECTION

We have considered the various possibilities of psychopathology in the religious mode of existence. We should like to conclude with a few remarks on the neurotic tendencies which we may discover in our daily efforts to reach religious perfection as it has been de-scribed in this book. To be sure, a whole new work could be devoted to this subject, but we shall have to restrict ourselves here to a summary of the main indications of such tendencies.

When I experience a strong need for affection and approval in my spiritual life, I should be suspicious about the wholesomeness of my motives. For example, I may feel a need to please those who are my spiritual directors or models, such as the priests of my parish, the clergyman who is the director of a religious organization to which I belong, my novice master or mistress, my superior or my fellow religious. I am anxious to live up to their expectations. What I imagine to be their expectation becomes far more important to me than the love of God, His expectation, and His merciful understanding of my weakness. Even my relation to God may be permeated by this neurotic need for approval of my religious performance. Then my spiritual joy is no longer based on my awareness of His redeeming love, which surrounds me in spite of my shortcomings, but on my conviction that I am successful in my spiritual life, for then I can imagine that God approves of me. I can even feel that my need for approval is fulfilled in a secret and mystical way by my invisible Master. Such an attitude is self-defeating, because I shall have to realize repeatedly that as a finite, sinful human being I can never hope to find infinite approval in the eyes of God. All that I can hope for is infinite mercy.

A spiritual life that is built on a striving after approval is bound to become a debacle. This longing for approval makes me extremely sensitive to rejection of any kind by anyone, but especially by persons who represent for me authority in religious matters. I may even be tempted to neglect what God desires of me for Himself and His Church if I feel that it might jeopardize the approval which I so sorely need. For example, if I am a Christian intellectual, I may resist the impulse of the Holy Spirit to explore new areas of religious knowledge. Such exploration may lead to error, and I may fear the "raised eyebrows" of wise men in authority who will be obliged to voice disapproval. Instead of listening to the Holy Spirit and accepting with a humble heart the risk of mistakes and of subsequent disapproval, I may listen only to my own need for affection and adulation. I may even go so far as to deceive myself with the rationalization that being perfect in the eyes of others is being perfect in the eyes of God. From this moment on, my spiritual life becomes a façade for man, but behind this front is no temple. I have lost my center of gravity in God as He reveals Himself in me. I have placed it in fellow men and in the good opinion which I desire them to have of me.

My obedience to religious authority should not be abused as an escape from the risk of responsibility in those areas which are left open to my free choice. I should be obedient; I should humbly accept both direction and disapproval; but I should not give in to neurotic anticipatory fear of disapproval which paralyzes in advance my initiative and activity. If I "play it safe," I shall make it impossible for any superior ever to find positive fault with my ideas or actions. Disapproval will be out of the question, not because of my supposed holiness, but because of the complete absence of energetic thought or dynamic action. No one can find fault with initiative that does not exist.

The neurotic need for approval may become a cultural disease. In this case, it is not impossible that an entire religious group within such a culture may be perverted by neuroticism and suffer from lack of creativity. In such a situation, no one dares to take the risk of responsibility. The life of each person is no longer motivated by self-forgetting love for God, but by a paralyzing fear of the possible disapproval of the person who is above him. This person in turn feels the same fear for the person to whom he is responsible, and so on through the whole line of command. In such a group, the spirit of the Lord is silenced by the spirit of fright. What results is a lifeless community of Christians who are no longer fearlessly involved in the work of God in this world, but in the defensive enterprise of safeguarding their positions within a closed power structure.

Another symptom of neurotic tendencies in my search for religious perfection may be my need for a clergyman, a confessor, a spiritual director, or a pious friend who is willing to assume full responsibility for my religious life. If I am a neurotic religious personality, I may try to live my spiritual life vicariously through another person. Not only do I expect him to be accountable for me and solve all my problems, but I also expect him to give me his full attention, love, and exclusive friendship. I dread being alone and deserted. I overemphasize the place of affection in my life, and I use spiritual direction unwittingly to secure this affection, instead of making it a means of personal growth in God's love alone. I expect love to solve all my problems, to soothe all my pains, to remove the burden of all responsibility.

Still another result of neurotic misunderstanding of spiritual life may be the restriction of my life within limits which are unreasonably narrow. I shall not demand anything even if I need it badly. I shall be content with as little as possible and make a fetish of being modest, unnoticed, and retiring. I may imagine that this attitude is the proof of unusual saintliness in me. However, a deeper analysis would reveal to me that this attitude is the result of my neurotic fear of failure of not being as successful as I would like to be, or of losing my halo of self-effacing modesty. If I were an authentic religious person, I would be willing to appear immodest or to bear the pain of the jealousy of others when the work of my Lord required that I take this risk, for His work would count more with me than my own acceptance as a saintly person in the eyes of others. When I do something creative for the Lord, I may threaten the quiet of others. Therefore, I shall evoke irritation and criticism. But if I am authentic in my spiritual life, I shall not escape this suffering by restricting my existence within a false modesty and a semi-retirement from life which would spare me criticism.

When my deepest drive for religious perfection is colored by neurotic tendencies, I may seek for power within the religious organization of which I am a member, as a layman, a priest, or a religious. I may crave power for its own sake, not for the sake of the religious community or of the faithful. Moreover, my personal spiritual life may be marked by my addiction to power. Religious perfection becomes for me perfect self-control in all situations, the absence of spontaneity and normal emotion. My dedication to the religious cause becomes dependent on its power to increase my hold on myself and on others. I am very careful about the nature of my religious occupation. I avoid under many pretexts any work that would not lead to an increase in my power or prestige. On the other hand, the same neurotic tendency may lead me to a dread of ambiguous, unexplored, risky situations which I cannot control immediately. Everything must be neat, well organized, safe, sure, and secure. Otherwise I feel frightened because control is for me the only means to make my world a safe place to live in.

The neurotic religious person is also frequently inclined to value people only in so far as they can be used for his own ends. Thus my "religious" love for people is an interest in them only in so far as they can satisfy my need for adulation, for popularity, and for veneration as a holy, wise, and understanding man. This neurotic symptom may lead me to surround myself with those Christian families, friends, and students who feel drawn by their own needs to admire, love, and adulate a priest, religious, or lay apostle. I then avoid as a plague those critical, outspoken Christians who do not hesitate to voice their dissatisfaction with me and with other representatives of the Church. If such a neurotic tendency spreads among large numbers of people, their Christianity may deteriorate into a mutual admiration society out of touch with reality. They may spend their lives singing lullabies, as it were, to one another. Such a Christianity may fall into a peaceful, sentimental slumber while others conquer the world.

My spiritual life may be poisoned by other neurotic ambitions. Because I feel insecure, for example, I need to surpass others in perfect religious behavior and apostolic activity. I feel satisfied only if I am the very best. I must always be the first in the chapel and the last to leave. I need to be the model of religious regularity that no one can surpass. When I study, I have to be the best student; when I speak, the best speaker; when I sing, the best singer. Above all, I have to feel that I am the most virtuous of all. Paradoxically, I must also be the most humble. Therefore, I am always advertising my humility, especially when I am praised by others. This joyful feeling of humility suddenly disappears, however, when others agree with me and doubt my virtue. I continually drive myself to increasing religious perfection and regularity, to more and more magnificent manifestations of apostolic fervor, in order to display my superiority in saintliness. Deep within me, however, I feel a neurotic insecurity, a fear of being insignificant and worthless. I battle this latent insecurity by steadily forcing myself to be the best. The source of my efforts is not my love of God, but overwhelming anxiety and the secret feeling of worthlessness at the root of my existence. Nevertheless, I may believe that my remarkable regularity is the fruit of holiness.

On the other hand, the same insecurity may evoke in me a craving for self-sufficiency and independence. I am so afraid of losing the little that I feel myself to be that I distrust any influence of others on my spiritual life. Moreover, I fear that familiarity with fellow Christians may expose my hidden frailty and weakness to them. I am inclined to protect myself against any overwhelming influence from the outside, and against any poor impression I may make on others, by the avoidance of familiar contacts. To be as aloof as possible becomes the source of my security as a perfect religious model. When this symptom spreads in a Christian group, it may lead to a general aloofness in all those people who have been taught to be splendid examples of religious and spiritual life. It may also lead to an aloof clergy which alienates itself from the common run of mankind, except for a small in-group of staunch admirers.

Finally, the neurotic perversion of the quest for religious perfection may reveal itself in the need to be without fault or blemish. I examine myself continually for possible flaws and imperfections, and I am deeply chagrined when I discover any temptation or failure. My greatest anxiety is that others may discover my human frailty. And my deepest insecurity makes it necessary for me to feel infallible, all-wise, all-holy, a model for all around me.

We all may discover in ourselves certain manifestations of neurotic tendencies. With the grace of God, we may gradually overcome them if they are not too deeply rooted in our lives. A frank and wise spiritual director may be of considerable help in the purification of our intentions. In exceptional cases, however, psychotherapy or professional counseling may be indicated. For this reason, Christianity has need today of specialists who are well trained in spirituality, psychology, and psychotherapy: men and women of deep and genuine spiritual life and of excellent psychological training who are willing to fulfill the humble role of John the Baptist to other Christians. They are not called to help people in the full flowering of their presence to Christ. They have the far more humble vocation of preparing the way for Christ by helping their fellow Christians to explore neurotic tendencies which poison their holy motives and cripple the development of their religious mode of existence.

BIBLIOGRAPHY

CALON, P. J. A., and J. J. G. PRICK, *Psychologische grondbegrippen.* Arnhem, Holland: Van Loghum Slaterus, 1962.

DONDEYNE, A., *Contemporary European Thought and Christian Faith.* Pittsburgh, Pa.: Duquesne University Press, 1958.

————, *Faith and the World.* Pittsburgh, Pa.: Duquesne University Press, 1963.

GURWITSCH, A., *Field of Consciousness.* Pittsburgh, Pa.: Duquesne University Press, 1964.

KWANT, R. C., *Encounter.* Pittsburgh, Pa.: Duquesne University Press, 1960.

————, *The Phenomenological Philosophy of Merleau-Ponty.* Pittsburgh, Pa.: Duquesne University Press, 1963.

LUIJPEN, W. A., *Existential Phenomenology.* Pittsburgh, Pa.: Duquesne University Press, 1960.

————, *Phenomenology and Atheism.* Pittsburgh, Pa.: Duquesne University Press, 1964.

MASLOW, A. H., *Motivation and Personality*. New York: Harper & Row, Publishers, 1954.

MAY, R., and A. VAN KAAM. "Existential Theory and Therapy," *Current Psychiatric Therapies*, Vol. III. New York: Grune & Stratton, Inc., 1963.

STRASSER, S., *Phenomenology and the Human Sciences*. Pittsburgh, Pa.: Duquesne University Press, 1963.

————, *The Soul in Metaphysical and Empirical Psychology*. Pittsburgh, Pa.: Duquesne University Press, 1957.

VAN KAAM, A. L., "Assumptions in Psychology," *Journal of Individual Psychology*, Vol. 14 (1958), 22-28.

————, "Clinical Implications of Heidegger's Concepts of Will, Decision, and Responsibility," *Review of Existential Psychology and Psychiatry* (Fall 1961), pp. 205-16.

————, "Commentary on 'Freedom and Responsibility Examined,'" *Behavioral Science and Guidance, Proposals and Perspectives*, eds. Ester Lloyd-Jones and Ester M. Westervelt. New York: Teachers College, Columbia University Press, 1963.

————, "Counseling and Existential Psychology," *Harvard Educational Review* (Fall 1962).

————, "Existential Psychology as a Theory of Personality," *Review of Existential Psychology and Psychiatry* (Winter 1963).

————, "The Fantasy of Romantic Love," *Modern Myths and Popular Fancies*. Pittsburgh, Pa.: Duquesne University Press, 1961.

————, "Freud and Anthropological Psychology," *The Justice* (Brandeis University) (May 1959).

————, "Humanistic Psychology and Culture," *Journal of Humanistic Psychology*, Vol. 1 (Spring 1961), 94-100.

————, "The Impact of Existential Phenomenology on the Psychological Literature of Western Europe," *Review of Existential Psychology and Psychiatry*, Vol. 1 (1961), 63-92.

————, *A Light to the Gentiles*. Detroit: Bruce Publishing Co., 1962.

————, "The Nurse in the Patient's World," *The American Journal of Nursing*, Vol. 59 (1959), 1708-10.

————, "Phenomenal Analysis: Exemplified by a Study of the Experience of 'Really Feeling Understood,'" *Journal of Individual Psychology*, Vol. 15 (1959), 66-72.

————, "A Psychology of the Catholic Intellectual," in *The Christian Intellectual* (Samuel Hazo, editor). Pittsburgh, Pa.: Duquesne University Press, 1963.

————, "A Psychology of Falling-Away-From-The-Faith," *Insight*, Vol. 2, No. 2 (Fall 1963), 3-17.

VAN KAAM, A. L., "Religion and Existential Will," *Insight,* Vol. 1, No. 1 (Summer 1962).

——, "Review of *The Divided Self* by R. D. Laing," *Review of Existential Psychology and Psychiatry* (Winter 1962), pp. 85-88.

——, "Sex and Existence," *Review of Existential Psychology and Psychiatry* (Spring 1963).

——, *The Third Force in European Psychology.* Greenville, Del.: Psychosynthesis Research Foundation, 1960.

——, *The Vocational Director and Counseling.* Derby, N.Y.: St. Paul Publications, 1962.

Index

INDEX

A

Abilities, 81-82
Acceptance, 2, 15, 58, 67, 157
Acclaim, 31
Administrators, 130
Affection, 68, 83, 106
Ambitions, 95, 158
Anger, 138
Anxiety, 34, 52, 70, 72, 74, 92, 95, 99, 102, 115, 118, 140, 145, 150, 152, 158-59
Apostolate, 114
Approval, 154-56
Asceticism, 116-17
Attachment, 18
Attitude, 40, 85
  assimilative, 23
  communicative, 24
  disparaging, 25
  evocative, 24
Awareness, 45, 115-17, 148, 150

B

Beauty, 77
Behavior, 22, 25, 27, 32-35, 53, 85, 103-4, 109, 130, 137-39, 143-44, 149, 153
Being, 120-21, 126, 129, 134-35, 148, 151
Bitterness, 82, 140
Body, 52, 54

C

Capacities, 70
Care, 141
Celibacy, 67, 83

Character, 85
Childishness, 36
Christ, 44, 55, 58-59, 73-74, 77
Commitment, 6-8, 19, 24, 28, 30, 47, 57, 77, 80, 120, 135-39
Competence, 59
Compulsion, 102, 118
Conflict, 25, 29, 38-40, 144, 154
Conformity, 65, 73, 148
Consistency, 56
Contrition, 26, 32, 102
Conventionality, 72-73
Counselor, 13
Creativeness, 78, 150
Culture, 12, 38-39, 71, 120, 124, 130, 132, 145-46, 150, 154, 156
Customs, 35, 66, 85, 92

D

Decision, 18-19, 23
Defeatism, 149
Defenses, 140
Dependence, 145
Depression, 149, 153
Despair, 33, 149, 151
Detachment, 18, 61, 76-78, 116
Determinism, 105
Development, 6, 50, 120, 122-23, 131, 152
Devotions, 31, 35, 63
Dialogue, 100, 113, 117
Differentiation, 4-5, 32, 119
Director, Spiritual, 60, 63, 115, 124, 156, 159
Discipline, 108
Discouragement, 88
Disobedience, 32
Distance, 51, 56, 76, 78, 116
Distrust, 140

Resentment, 95
Resistance, 39, 138
Respect, 84
Responsibility, 36, 48, 99, 101-2, 104, 117, 155-56
Revelation, 98, 112, 117

S

Sacrifice, 36
Scrupulosity, 118
Security, 60, 158
Self, 145, 147-48, 151
  acceptance, 46
  actualization, 19, 134
  awareness, 39, 44-45, 115
  centeredness, 70, 135
  consciousness, 44
  control, 157
  deception, 9
  determination, 47
  experience, 44, 48
  fulfillment, 56
  integration, 17, 45
  realization, 12, 46, 80, 134
  rejection, 151, 153
  sufficient, 46
  understanding, 37, 79
Selfishness, 46
Sensuousness, 8
Serenity, 129
Shame, 115
Silence, 56, 60, 95
Simplicity, 74
Sin, 14, 26, 101-2, 104
Situation, 12, 15-17, 32, 34, 46, 49, 54, 58, 80, 83, 97-99, 106, 109, 115, 139
Skills, 147
Spirit, ecumenical, 62
Spirituality, 35
Spontaneity, 74, 113-15, 117, 150, 157
Stability, 51, 53-55, 60
Superior, 124
Surrender, 139
Symbols, 39, 126, 130-31
Syncretism, 63

T

Talent, 82-83
Teacher, 124-25

Techniques, 146
Temperament, 85-86
Temptation, 138, 159
Tensions, 5, 25, 32, 118, 145-46, 150-51, 154
Timidity, 74
Tolerance, 122
Traditions, 147, 150
Transcendence, 2, 39, 58, 65, 72, 80, 136, 138-41, 151, 153
Transference, 126-27, 145-46
  demonizing, 126-27, 145
  existential, 121, 123-30, 132
  idolizing, 126-27, 145
  narcissistic, 121-23
  negative, 126-28, 132, 145
  original, 124-25
  positive, 123, 126-27
  secondary, 125
Trust, 2-3, 14, 34, 122, 124

U

Unconscious, 21, 148-49
Uniqueness, 44-46, 58, 79
Unity, 45

V

Values, 20, 66, 147, 149, 152
  hierarchy of, 69, 125, 128
Vocation, 44, 107

W

Weakness, 138
Wholeness, 49
Will, 3, 51, 80, 89, 92-93, 98-99, 101, 103, 105, 108-9, 112-18
  existential, 92, 108, 112, 116-17
  God's, 10-11, 28, 30
  religious, 106, 108, 111-13
  willfulness, 92, 95-96, 98, 118
  will-lessness, 99-101, 118
Wisdom, 94
Wishes, 113
World, 38, 80, 126, 146-47
  existential, 22, 62
  my world, 115
  of meaning, 4, 24-25, 35, 39, 137